# Fashion Advertising and Promotion

### PROFESSOR ARTHUR A. WINTERS
Chairman: Advertising and Communications Department
Fashion Institute of Technology State University of New York

### STANLEY GOODMAN
Former Professor: Advertising and Communications Department
Fashion Institute of Technology/State University of New York

## FIFTH EDITION

FAIRCHILD PUBLICATIONS, NEW YORK

# ACKNOWLEDGMENTS

The subject matter in this book was organized by the authors. The development of its contents and approach, however, is the result of a continuing exchange of experience and viewpoints with our colleagues in the departments of Advertising and Communications, and Fashion Buying and Merchandising of the Fashion Institute of Technology. Their evaluations and recommendations have been constructive and valuable.

We have had the splendid cooperation of our many colleagues in advertising and marketing education; and from professionals in media, retail advertising and promotion, public relations, and advertising agencies. We appreciate their permission to reproduce much of the material used for demonstration and illustration in this book.

Our own F.I.T. students have added enormously to the various discussions by their questions, challenges, and most gratifying of all, by their contributions to our knowledge as professionals pursuing their careers in fashion advertising and promotion.

The authors also acknowledge the efforts of Nancy Kurz, F.I.T. staff member; our illustrator and designer, Barbara Scholey; and our editor, Olga Kontzias.

# Preface

What makes this business of fashion advertising and promotion so different? The main difference between "fashion promotion" and "non-fashion promotion" is the nature of the *product* involved. Fashion is much more than the clothing which you put on your back. It is part of an individual's inner concept of self. It is a reflection of history, culture, the arts, and human behavior. It is also big business in our economy. This book is concerned with advertising and promoting fashion. It deals with concepts and terminology which are relevant to the sales promotion of fashion on each of its levels of selling. Fashion promotion activities are initiated by primary producers promoting raw materials to retailers; apparel manufacturers promoting to retailers; and retailers promoting to the consumer.

The purpose of this book is to help make discussions in fashion advertising and promotion meaningful. This book has been designed to encourage the reader to raise provocative questions for discussion.

It is hoped that these pages can provide the student with the kind of basic background information which will enable an instructor to devote more time to workshop exercises designed to develop skills in evaluating and criticizing fashion advertising and promotion.

We believe that students should *learn by doing*. We have written with this objective in mind—to help the instructor make a course of study in Fashion Advertising and Promotion a "do" course. Such a course may be designed to aid the student in developing a competency to evaluate whether an advertisement, a window display, a special event, or a promotional program has had adequate planning and execution . . . why it is likely to be effective or ineffective, appropriate or ill-chosen. This is equally as important for the fashion merchandising and buying student as it is for the student of fashion advertising and promotion.

In recent years there has been considerable propaganda about advertising and promotion as being the sinister plot of "hidden persuaders" and of the "Madison Avenue Boys." All advertising and promotion are not evil. All advertising executives are not dishonest, any more than all doctors, lawyers, teachers, or politicians. In advertising there is always the marketplace. This is where the promotional conniver meets his doom. The consumer has a healthy habit of coming back for more only when the merchant's promise is delivered and satisfaction is enjoyed. In addition, the power of competition exacts increasing demands for such satisfaction.

It has been wisely said that, ". . . nothing happens until something is sold." The processes and actions that advertise and promote the sale of fashion, textiles and apparel . . . how they work and the criteria to analyze and evaluate them . . . these are the subjects of this book.

Stanley Goodman                          Arthur A. Winters
Boca Raton, Florida                      New York, New York
1978

# Contents

# 1

# The Excitement
# of Fashion As A Product
# and An Inner Concept

Two attractive women are busy shopping in a supermarket. You might not guess that they are mother and daughter. They are Phoebe Smith and her eighteen-year old daughter, Sue. They are both dressed for supermarket shopping . . . well, not exactly. They are attired in much the same way as many women who go shopping —in very short smart tennis dresses. And we mean to say *short,* for a considerable exposure of their derrières and panties is evident.

This is no lack of modesty; it is fashion. Tennis clothes are fashion. We may question if all those who wear these special and often expensive styles are really tennis buffs, or are they satisfied to merely give that impression? These could be the same women who just a few years ago would never have accepted *hot pants,* a brief fad for *very* short shorts. Hot pants were never quite so revealing as most of the tennis dresses. When fashion makes a look or style acceptable, mere modesty becomes unimportant.

Men as well as women are wearing tennis garb both on and off the court. Tennis is one of the games people play on and off the court, and its wave of popularity dictates the manner of dress. The active and fashion tenniswear togs business alone has exceeded the $250-million mark, and is still growing.

The lowly sneaker, a rubber-soled canvas shoe that for years sold for two or three dollars a pair, has moved up in the fashion cycle right along with tennis. The price has also increased. Sneakers have become a status symbol with brand names and identifying stripes and styles. Recent additions to this trend include all forms of warm-up suits, athletic uniforms, and accessories which sport popular team motifs. The day of the "jock" (super-athlete) also has its reflection in popular fashion.

Fashion is that fickle, fleeting, flattering phenomenon which promises to sell moods as well as merchandise. How to present a fashion, develop a demand for it, and sell it are professional processes. The uninitiated and amateur can be overwhelmed by the professional whose knowledge and techniques are employed in the effective promotion of different kinds of products.

How many people in this country wear out their clothing? An item of clothing is rarely discarded because of wear; but it may go out-of-fashion. After an outfit has been seen several times, it often goes into retirement at the back of a closet. Then there are such purchases as the "drop-dead" dress. This is a dress that a woman buys specifically for a special social function, and on her entrance, she hopes that every other woman in the room drops dead with envy . . . unless of course the dress has already arrived . . . on another woman. Bare chest exposure is an attention-getting fashion for both women and men. The wearing of unusual body jewelry has developed a cult among men . . . fashion accessories, hats, scarves, and hair styles are intended to command attention, and certainly do!

Fashion is excitement. We are seeing more and more of it in the current advertising, display (visual merchandising), and promotional activities. Fashion is fantasy, role playing, and self-concept. Clothing can be used to command attention and secure admiration from our peers. Personal fashion expression can be exemplified by a woman in the supermarket doing her shopping in a scant tennis dress.

## THE NATURE OF FASHION

### WHAT IS FASHION?

If one wants to promote fashion, one cannot avoid being very much involved with the psychology of fashion expression, individual satisfaction, and consumer behavior. Throughout this book, finding out about fashion advertising and promotion is finding out how each of the various promotion activities work individually and in combination to sell fashion. It is important to know what it is that one is promoting when he promotes fashion. It is important to consider what the fashion product really means to all the individuals who want it.

It has often been said that fashion is like any other product that you are attempting to sell. This is basically true because in one way fashion can be considered a product, such as wine or suntan lotion. Fashion products have certain characteristics and features which can be identified—but when you really try to compare fashion with other products you run into difficulties. Even those who are in the business of selling fashion cannot always agree on what it is.

Recently one department store president said, "Fashion no longer exists." Another defined it as being ". . . life-style statements" and a third said "Art on your back, or in your home, or personal life—that's fashion." And another said: "Fashion is nothing but a lot of non-sense." Four diverse and somewhat generalized points of view on the same product—fashion.

## FASHION—IS IT A PRODUCT OR A CONCEPT?

Since you are going to be concerned with promoting or selling fashion, it makes sense that you have a viewpoint on this unusual product. Why has it the power of doing so much for people? Why is it probably as much of a *concept* as it is a product. You might first ask yourself "What is fashion to me?" Is it the jeans I'm wearing, the eye makeup I put on, the new poster I bought, the costumes in the play I just saw, the bedspread on my bed? Could it be all these things and much more?

A student of fashion marketing most likely would recognize the name of Emilio Pucci. His name is well known in the world of fashion, and he is one of the pioneer creators of fashions in textile design. He has this to say about fashion:

> Today what once concerned a minority has become a matter
> of general interest. Not only in clothing but in all expres-
> sions of contemporary living, from architecture to interior
> decoration, from the auto to the refrigerator, the pervasive

influence of television, magazines, and fast, easy transportation have made fashion today one of the determining factors in civilized living.

Pucci makes fashion a pretty important sounding product as well as an aspect of human behavior. The importance of style or life-style, of taste, of aesthetics in our lives cannot be overrated. Fashion is finally being recognized as a basic human need for *personal expression.* Let us examine it a little more closely.

In its broadest sense, fashion has been defined as all outward manifestations of civilized behavior which receive general acceptance for a limited period of time. These include moral standards, table manners, car design, as well as dress. This defines fashion as indeed an enormously universal product and concept—which touches every facet of our lives. But, if someone says to you: "Quick, tell me what is fashion," . . . chances are you would think in terms of apparel. And this is natural because fashion in a personal sense is reflected in the way you dress. Some fashion writers define fashion as an extension of one's personality. It is often used to emphasize or deemphasize one's personality. Some people dress *up* to communicate the message "I'm better than I really am" or *down* "This is what I am not, but have to be." Another example is the junior executive who is complying with the image of his conservative boss by dressing up in a vested, pin-stripe suit and a sincere tie. What is a sincere tie? It is a traditional understated combination of color, designs, and patterns which symbolize conservative tastes.

It is impossible for anyone not to use some phase of non-verbal language in the way they dress. Colors, silhouette, patterns, and fabrics speak for you before you even open your mouth.

Fashion can be the way men and women express certain ideas about themselves and about the world in general—and a way they can do this very directly is by the clothes they wear. The best current example of this self-expression would be the ubiquitous blue jeans. If you decorate them you show the world how creative you are. If you wear them to work you are trying to show you are liberated. If you like them tattered, chances are, that psychologically speaking, you are expressing something you do not like about excessive neatness. But, the fact that you are wearing jeans or denims at all means first that you are *in* fashion, and that you are using that fashion to express something about yourself and about the times you live in.

## FASHION MIRRORS SOCIETY

This idea of fashion as self-expression leads to the concept that in many ways fashion tells us certain things about our society and its structures.

Fashion is not only an expression of the individual but also of the world he or she lives in. Fashion, according to the late, noted costume historian, James Laver, is definitely not an arbitrary phenomenon: It can be made to reveal its elusive character if we realize it is related to, and reflective of historical and social events in at least four significant ways—politically, economically, culturally, and sexually. To understand these relationships we just have to look at some familiar examples.

Christian Dior's New Look, which was launched in 1947, is one of the best-known examples of fashion relating to and mirroring *politics.* The years before 1947 were the years of World War II. The *look* for women was uniforms with their short, practical economical tubular skirts, and padded masculine shoulders. This look was drab, unromantic, unfeminine. With the end of the war came Dior's dramatic lengthening of skirts, with an emphasis on the bosom and the waist. Dior said of it, "We had behind us a time of war, of uniforms, of women in the services with broad shoulders like a boxer's. I sketched flower-like women, gently curved shoulders, rounded breasts and reed-slim waists and skirts that spread out like flower petals."

Politics ended the war. Dior was astute enough to realize what women wanted when it was over: A return to femininity, a feeling for romance and luxury.

In its feeling for luxury and elegance Dior's New Look is also an example of the way fashion relates to *economics.* The war years were full of rationing, hardship, and poverty. Once they were over there was a need to recover some of the luxuries that had existed before the war. A direct way of expressing a reaction against poverty might be a skirt full of fabric, worn over sheer nylon stockings, a look that Dior said was decidedly not very practical—it was a look that was like a flower.

You may also recognize that habits of dress are part of a *cultural* legacy—in the sense that certain groups will maintain, with only slight periodic refinements, a standard of attire considered appropriate for their "class." The Brooks Brothers look for men is considered proper dress for certain professional and business groups. The single-breasted, three-button suit; white or light blue shirt; and a low-key tie has been a classic form of attire throughout many other changes in fashion trends.

The fourth and most important way that fashion mirrors society is *sexually,* and we are seeing an enormous emphasis on this aspect at the present time. When the moral standards of a society become more permissive it becomes permissible to show more parts of the body and this is precisely what started to happen in the mid-60's with Rudi Gernreich's see-through blouses and topless bathing suits and Courrèges' mini-skirted, space-child look. There are fashion authorities who believe that changes in fashion can be traced to the S.E.Z. principle—the Shifting Erogenous Zone. It is generally agreed that one of the basic functions of fashion is to increase the erotic appeal of the female body by constantly shifting emphasis from one part of it to another. So you will find that at one discreet period waists are the center of attraction, then when times change, the emphasis changes to the legs, and changes again to the thighs and breasts.

## FASHION AS DICTATOR—HAS THE DICTATOR DIED?

We have just examined four ways that fashion is intrinsically related to society and its changes in attitude and expression. But we still do not have a complete picture of fashion as a concept and a product until we have examined it historically—for if fashion is a product you are going to advertise and promote, you have to know something about how people tried to sell it in the past. And the recent past will be what concerns us here.

Time was when women were submissive and subservient—they stayed at home, took care of children and husbands, and for the most part did what they were told. Fashion was a matter of you are what you wear—and you wear what you are told. These were the times of the great god-voice Fashion, dating from the Twenties. In the Sixties one of the Fashion Voices was the Diana Vreeland voice, who as chief editor of *Vogue* Magazine said things like, "Navy blue is the new black,"— and just like that, there were little basic blue dresses where there had been basic black. Dior had said there was a New

Look—women snapped it up—but *you* know that Dior was not just being a dictator, he was very intelligent in sensing that the time was right for his decree. Nevertheless, women were followers in fashion as well as in their own private lives. Then along came Betty Friedan and the "Feminine Mystique," Gloria Steinem and the Women's Liberation Movement, Radical Feminists, and "Ban the Bra." Women seemed to start thinking for themselves. The feminists said that fashion was frivolous, fashion was dead, fashion was a product no more. But, was it really all over for fashion? Definitely and emphatically not! Women would not do away with an expression as vital as the clothes on their backs—and those clothes were and are *fashion.* What they could do away with however, was the dictatorial voice, the you-wear-what-you're-told business.

So it became clear by the late Sixties that you could no longer sell your product by the dictatorial method. Women were not going to automatically adopt the New Look, the Old Look, the Maxi Look, or the Peasant Look just because the fashion magazines and newspapers and stores said it was the greatest thing that ever happened. Women really started thinking for themselves, and their liberation may have sparked a men's fashion liberation. The late Sixties and the Seventies have seen a return to the "way of the peacock." Many men have added to their wardrobe of business suits and sincere ties, several versions of casual, leisure-style sportswear separates formerly worn only on weekends.

Those who sell fashion must develop a perceptive skill in knowing what consumers will accept—what they need and want; their sense of *timing* must be responsive to all the signals being sent out by their audience. They know that fashion success is determined by the acceptance of those who wear it. Textile designers and apparel designers apply their multi-talents to creating what the liberated *and* the non-liberated want for their particular styles of living. If the creators of apparel have provided what people want and need, then the fashion promoters can give consumers reasons to buy, based on these wants and needs. In light of our previous discussion, can you think of any manufactured product which is of more personal importance to people than clothing? Is there anything we can buy which can come closer to creating an inner-concept of ourselves, which we would like others to see? Promoting fashion is selling clothing to people who want or need it for very human reasons.

Motivating customers to respond to a product as personal as fashion is about the most exciting challenge a promoter can face.

## WHAT THIS BOOK IS ABOUT . . .

The purpose of Advertising and Promotion in the fashion industry, and the procedures, methods, and techniques used in the various promotional activities, are the topics of this book. The special *language* of advertising and promotion and its specific applications to fashion is also important. We recommend the *Glossary* on page 226 as an aid to the understanding of any term which the text does not explain at the time.

Change is a most important factor in fashion and involves every level of the business. Fashion sales promotion itself is no exception to this factor of change. Historically the fashion business has been production-oriented. Designing and making the product have been the areas of greatest interest. There remain a few staunch believers in this attitude. The new breed of executives, however, is in the process of developing a more marketing-oriented approach to the fashion business. They feel that equal emphasis must be assigned to market research, consumer research, merchandising and to distribution, along with attention to product research and development, design and production.

Because the large retailer, the department store, is an excellent example of a firm in the fashion business which utilizes a comprehensive and coordinated Sales Promotion Program, we will use many examples of how such retailers use advertising and promotion activities to sell merchandise and ideas. The principles involved will be the same for other levels in the industry; e.g., producers of raw materials and manufacturers of apparel and accessories. Where differences occur, these variations will be noted and discussed. Sales Promotion specialists generally agree that the "moment of truth" for evaluating the effectiveness of sales promotion occurs at the retail level or *point-of-sale.* No firm, *on any level* in the fashion business, can claim success until the ultimate consumer says "yes." For this reason, a great deal of fashion promotion is retail or consumer-oriented. The processes and action that move fashion merchandise—how they work, how to evaluate them—these are the subjects of this book.

# 2

## The What, Why, Who, and What-for of Fashion Promotion

### FASHION SALES PROMOTION— A LANGUAGE OF ITS OWN

When a plumber thinks of a tight joint, he does not have in mind a saloon where the drinks are skimpy, any more than a carpenter thinks of a T-square as an old lady who sips tea. And so in the fashion business a knowledge of the specialized language of the field is necessary for those who wish to communicate with their co-workers or with their customers.

For example, one important point which might be remembered by a fashion writer is that the language differs radically in relation to the audience. A "line-for-line copy" of a French couturier's design would be completely understandable to the consumer. A "knock-off" of the very same item would be strictly the trade term for this merchandise. Except for those in the few major fashion centers, there would be a limited public outside the industry who would know such trade terms.

The language varies within the fashion field because there are so many individuals engaged in various promotion levels of the industry who have developed terms which emphasize the importance of their particular contribution to the whole process. It would be useful to note here that the use of the terms "Sales Promotion," "Promotion," and (to feature its best-known activity) *"Advertising* and *Promotion"* are relatively interchangeable. They are all *umbrella* terms which refer to all of the promotion activities: advertising, display, publicity, fashion shows, and special events.

## WHAT IS SALES PROMOTION?

As previously mentioned, the interchanging of the definitions of such basic terms as Sales Promotion, Advertising and Promotion, or simply, Promotion, has been much abused and misused. There are almost as many definitions for Sales Promotion as there are sales promotion practitioners. It all depends upon whom you ask. Retailers, manufacturers, and advertising agencies each have their own version. Manufacturers regard sales promotion as a supplement to *personal* selling, which would classify all *nonpersonal* selling as promotion; advertising. agencies believe that sales promotion includes those collateral materials which "merchandise the advertising." They emphasize those aspects which complement their own philosophy of doing business. It is usually the retailer who thinks of sales promotion as an all-inclusive effort which coordinates all activities that contribute to generate profitable sales.

If we think of Sales Promotion in its broadest sense, it may include *any* activity, *personal* or *nonpersonal,* which is used to influence the sale of merchandise services or ideas.* See Figure 1 for a graphic representation of Sales Promotion activities in a retail store.

THE NONPERSONAL SELLING ACTIVITIES

ADVERTISING—A nonpersonal method of influencing sales by sending a sponsored and paid message through mass media to a mass audience of potential customers.

DISPLAY (VISUAL MERCHANDISING)—A nonpersonal physical presentation of merchandise or ideas at the point-of-sale. It includes window, exterior, interior, and remote display.

PUBLICITY—An unsigned and nonpaid commentary, verbal or written, in public information media. It is stimulated by interested

*Marketing Definitions,* American Marketing Association (Chicago, 1960), page 18.

10

*Figure 1. Sales promotion activities and media which are used to bring the customer to the point-of-sale and personal selling in a department and specialty store.*

parties seeking to present news about a company, its products, policies, personnel, activities or services.

SPECIAL EVENTS—Specific devices, features, services, sales inducements, exhibits, demonstrations, and attractions which influence the sale of merchandise or ideas.

FASHION SHOWS—Presentations of merchandise in living and moving form.

**THE PERSONAL SELLING ACTIVITY**

An oral presentation in conversation with a prospective customer for the purpose of making a sale of merchandise, services or ideas.

For the balance of our discussion, we will refer to all of the aforementioned activities as *Sales Promotion* or *Promotion,* or to emphasize its most prominent activity, *Advertising* and *Promotion.*

11

## WHY IS SALES PROMOTION IMPORTANT?

All businesses engage in some form of sales promotion activity. However, the terms used to describe their activities and methods employed by firms executing them may differ. With the advent of size and diversification of operations in the fashion business, the coordination of sales promotion activities becomes a vital function. Competition has never been more keen, nor markets more complex. Customers must be sold and continue to be sold if a business wishes to make a profit and to stay in business. It is for these reasons that sales promotion becomes an essential concern of top management.

The scope and responsibility of sales promotion in the fashion industry widens and deepens day by day. As business becomes more competitive, and customers become more selective, firms are using an increasing variety of public information media to promote through advertising and publicity. Each company must consider itself a communications center—especially the retailer. Greater emphasis is being placed on the use of a more effective "media-mix" of advertising in newspapers, direct mail, radio and television. Visual merchandising in window and interior displays which can sell merchandise and stimulate awareness of fashion themes is being used in surprising new ways. There is an ever-increasing use of publicity programs and community-inspired special events designed to sell products and ideas. The necessity for selling in every medium and from every vantage point, reaching out to where the customers are, is an accepted fact of business life. The fashion industry, one of the largest in our economy, must communicate on *every level* to maintain its position.

## WHO IS INVOLVED IN PROMOTING FASHION?

For our purposes, we shall classify firms in the fashion industry as either *producers, manufacturers* or *retailers* of clothing. The producers refer to the manufacturers of raw materials and the manufacturers refer to the "wholesalers" of finished apparel. The retailers distribute finished apparel to consumers. They are all involved in promoting fashion.

At every level in the marketing of fashion, *someone is selling.* His customer is the purchaser in the company next in line in the mar-

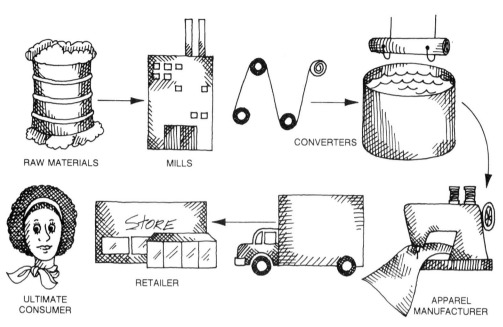

RAW MATERIALS

MILLS

CONVERTERS

STORE

RETAILER

ULTIMATE CONSUMER

APPAREL MANUFACTURER

*Figure 2. The "Marketing Process"—From raw materials producer to apparel manufacturer to retailer to ultimate consumer.*

keting process (see Figure 2). Farmers sell their natural fibers (cotton, wool), and chemical plants sell their man-made fibers to textile mills. The mills spin, weave or knit fiber into finished or unfinished fabric. Fabrics are sold as "gray goods" to converters who bleach, dye and finish them for sale to apparel manufacturers. The clothing manufacturer designs and produces finished apparel which he sells to the retailer. The retailer sells to the ultimate consumer. The whole process of selling on all of these market levels is a creative science to be studied and an art to be practiced. Those who perfect it are professionals. They are skilled practitioners in the science of showing customers how *they* can benefit from buying a specific product or accepting an idea. The professional salesperson does not use the "big pitch" or puffed-up words to overwhelm unwilling customers. He is a master salesperson rather than a super salesperson. He is not, on the other hand, a mere order-taker. The salesperson's depth of knowledge of the benefits of his product and the needs and wants of his customer are his equipment for success.

## THE "WHAT-FOR" (OR GENERAL OBJECTIVES) OF SALES PROMOTION

The fashion firm interested in selling its customers has a varied choice of ammunition, each designed to hit the target in a special way, at a different point and with its own distinctive impact. Each activity was developed because it helps to sell certain customers at certain times in a certain way which others cannot do—or do as well. The characteristics of each sales promotion activity were developed as a supplement and a complement to the basic one, *personal* selling. The *nonpersonal* activities were developed primarily because of the need to reach mass audiences.

### GENERAL OBJECTIVES

The common denominators of all sales promotion activities are their *General Objectives:*
   1. Selling a product, service or idea at a profit
   2. Building customer loyalty
   3. Generating interest
   4. Disseminating information

It is a matter of record that many companies which were too interested in *product* objectives (#1), and neglected *institutional* objectives (#2, #3, #4) are no longer around. Selling a product at a good profit is necessary if a firm is to do well in business. But building a positive institutional reputation and maintaining consumer patronage is insurance for staying in business.

### SPECIFIC PURPOSES OF SALES PROMOTION

General objectives of sales promotion are identical for any of the firms engaged in selling to each other or in promoting to the consumer. All businesses are interested in selling products, services or ideas at a profit. They should also be concerned with keeping their customers sold, stimulating customers' interest in new products and techniques, distributing information of use to customers. Each sales promotion program may reflect a particular strategy designed to meet specific problems affecting the selling of their products. Of the hundreds of different purposes for which sales promotion has been used, there are certain ones which form the basis for advertisements, displays, special events and publicity. These are used by all levels in the fashion industry. *Any specific use of sales promotion could satisfy one or more of its general objectives.*

For example: A retailer's advertisement about an improved product in a newspaper may be designed for the specific purpose of increasing the *frequency of replacement.* This will satisfy *general objective* ( #1): selling a product, service or idea.

A news story about new automated shipping methods could be released by a dress manufacturer to a trade publication such as *Women's Wear Daily (WWD),* to make this organization known to buyers. This also satisfies *general objective #* 1; in this case we are selling an *idea.*

The most typical *specific* purposes of sales promotion activities are as follows:

1. To introduce new products.
2. To indicate depth, range, and variety of product assortments.
3. To present special merchandise offers.
4. To bring related products together.
5. To attract new groups of customers.
6. To identify and differentiate brands and/or institutions.
7. To present special prices or conditions of sale.
8. To introduce special themes or events.
9. To make known the organization, departments, or personnel behind products.
10. To prevent substitution.
11. To establish fashion authority and leadership.
12. To render public or community service.
13. To give useful instruction or demonstration on the optimum use of a product.
14. To reach persons who influence the purchaser.

The exact nature of these specific purposes varies from firm to firm and from product to product. The particular selection of specific purposes of sales promotion depends upon which *general* objective of sales promotion seems most important at the time. This list is by no means complete. The sales promoter may have specific uses for sales promotion which would not be included on a list of typical specific purposes.

## THE LEVELS OF SELLING

The process of selling in the fashion industry involves many different types of firms selling to each other and *all of them promoting to the ultimate consumer.* It is important to realize that raw material producers and manufacturers of finished fashion products as well as retailers promote products and ideas to the ultimate consumer. We have previously stated that the four general objectives in any case are all the same—with specific uses designed to accomplish those objectives.

The *levels of selling* which occur between the different types of firms in the fashion industry, and between each type of firm and the consumer, have characteristic labels. These are:

1. Trade
2. National
3. Retail

*Market level* refers to the different firms in the fashion industry:

PRIMARY—The producers of fibers, textiles, linings, trimmings and other raw materials used in the manufacture of fashion apparel and accessories.

SECONDARY—The "wholesaler," "cutter," or apparel manufacturer of finished apparel and accessories.

RETAIL—The dealer or distributor of finished apparel and accessories to the ultimate consumer.

The key to understanding market level and level of selling is contained in the following:

*Who* is selling *what* to *whom* and for *which* reason?

An example of this would be: A producer of raw materials (WHO), selling a fabric (WHAT), to a sportswear manufacturer (WHOM), for the manufacture of ready-to-wear (WHICH reason). This level of selling is referred to as *trade sales promotion.* If the activity used in this case is advertising, we call this *trade advertising.* Figure 3 illustrates the different *levels* of selling.

When apparel manufacturers promote the sale of their apparel to retailers, this is also called *trade* sales promotion.

The retailer in selling to the ultimate consumer is involved in

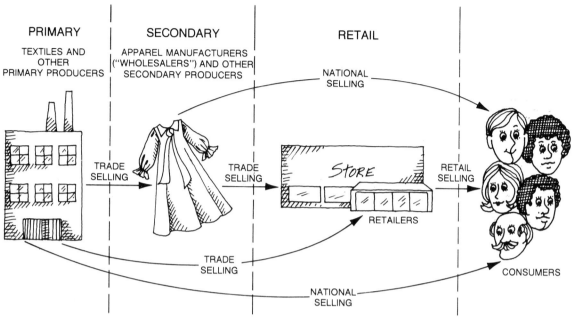

*Figure 3. The levels of selling in the fashion industry.*

*retail* sales promotion—his advertising is called *retail advertising;* his display, retail display.

Although the retailer has the most direct contact in selling merchandise to the ultimate consumer, producers and manufacturers also promote to consumers. This level of selling is referred to as *national* sales promotion. This is the promotion by producers and manufacturers of brand-identified products, addressed to consumers, who are being urged to buy from retailers who carry these branded products. A purpose of this form of selling is to establish an apparel manufacturer's identity and value of his products in the mind of the consumer. National sales promotion also occurs when a raw materials producer promotes his product-within-a-product to the consumer. The raw materials producer is saying to consumers: *"Buy brand-name dresses with 'my name-fabric' at leading stores."* The apparel manufacturer is saying: *"Buy my 'brand name dresses' at leading stores."* This is sometimes referred to as *pre-selling* the consumer.

The term national does not necessarily mean nationwide. It has a special meaning in actual practice. It does not refer to the *geographical* extent of promotion, or to its *quantity.* It refers rather to advertising and promotion from a producer or manufacturer to the ultimate consumer. In this case the audience of consumers could be in one city or state.

## WHO IS RESPONSIBLE FOR SALES PROMOTION?

### RETAIL

The responsibility for selling differs in various types of firms in the

*Figure 4. Can you identify which level of selling is represented by this advertisement? Who is selling what to whom?*

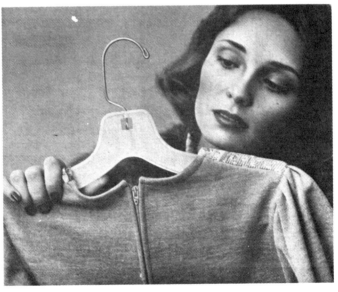

fashion industry. In most large department and specialty stores*, merchandise managers and buyers have varying degrees of responsibility for selling as well as buying ("what is bought, must be sold"). They share this responsibility with sales promotion directors, advertising and publicity managers.

Just sharing responsibility is not enough. One should understand the other person's job to some extent. Just what is he or she trying to do; and why. An important objective of this book is to offer some understanding of how merchandising and sales promotion people work together. Not everyone will g : the opportunity to observe what goes on in other departments. A buyer or floor supervisor should have knowledge of sales promotion and how it works. A sales promotion practitioner should be familiar with buying and merchandising procedure.

In larger retail organizations where there is a buyer and/or executive training program, an essential part of the "curriculum" would be experiences to develop familiarity with various phases of the retail operation. This means practical work experience in as many components of store operations as is feasible and pertinent to the trainee's career direction. Not every store offers such broad training. Regardless of where one works in a fashion organization, it is truly important to know how merchandise gets promoted and sold. That means among other things, a thorough knowledge of the activities of fashion advertising and promotion.

## MANUFACTURING

In manufacturing organizations, there are executives and managers whose major responsibility is the supervision of selling and salespeople. Here too, personal selling is supplemented by the other sales promotion activities. Sales promotion directors supervise advertising managers, publicity and display directors whose departments create and execute their parts of the Sales Promotion Program. The concept of professional sales management is essential to both the manufacturing and retailing firm in the fashion business.

---

*Many of the larger retail and retail chain organizations have separated the buying and selling functions, and employ professional sales managers to supervise salespeople. The buyer in most instances is the overall supervisor and consequently, has the basic responsibility for "what is bought, must be sold."

*Figure 5. Which of the two ads in Figures 5 and 6 is the national ad? How can you tell?*

*Figure 6. What are the identifying characteristics of the level of selling which this ad represents?*

It could be noted that manufacturer sales executives with their total concentration on the sciences of marketing and sales promotion may have developed their skills more comprehensively than retail merchandise managers and buyers who consider buying rather than selling as the major part of their jobs.

The most forward-thinking retailers are now instituting formal marketing research. This is designed to add to their knowledge of customers and consequently, to their effectiveness in promoting the sale of fashion.

## ORGANIZATION OF THE SALES PROMOTION RESPONSIBILITY

In those companies which have a sales promotion department, the sales promotion manager generally works closely with the sales department and/or merchandise divisions. Regardless of whom he reports to, the sales promotion manager must develop a coordinated program. In firms where there is no sales promotion department, the sales promotion function may be handled by the sales department. In some companies sales promotion planning and implementation are handled by external advertising agencies. However, no matter how the sales promotion responsibility is set up in a firm, the way it is planned and executed is of greater importance than are the particular staff and line organization.

The important thing is that sales promotion activities be considered an integral part of the planning of coordinated marketing programs. When sales promotion activities are not coordinated, the whole progress of marketing campaigns may be hindered by the lack of follow-through selling activity.

The responsibility of the sales promotion function is to bring about coordination and sales effectiveness. It should, therefore, be reviewed and planned as an essential part of a business' overall marketing effort—not as an adjunct or supplement.

In the fashion industry, manufacturers and retailers have organized their marketing and sales promotion efforts in whatever manner suits their individual marketing strategy. Sales promotion must:

1. Be *planned* with specific goals and objectives clearly spelled out.
2. *Select* the products to be promoted, prices, timing.
3. *Choose, coordinate* and *execute* the particular sales promotion activities most consistent with company policy and most

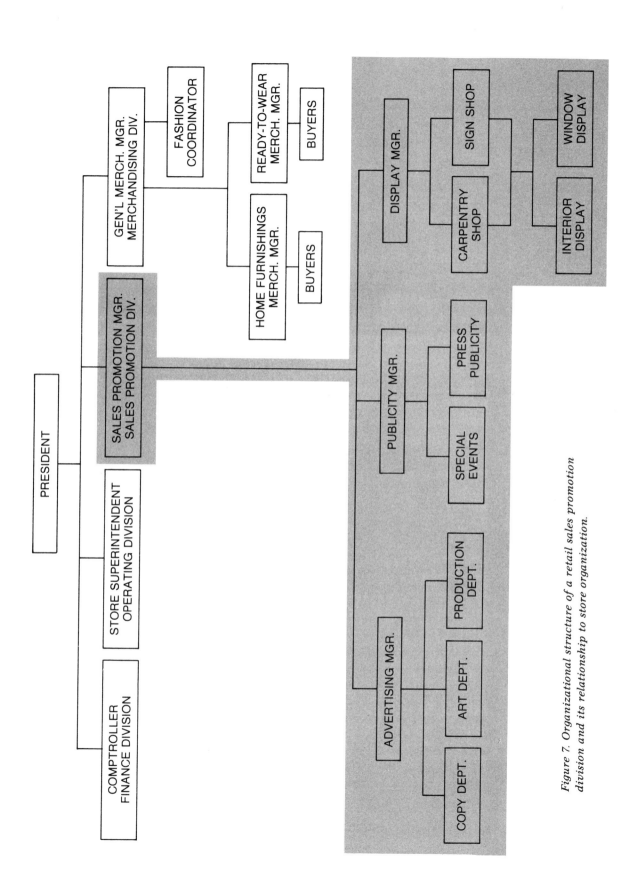

Figure 7. Organizational structure of a retail sales promotion division and its relationship to store organization.

likely to realize specific objectives and long range goals. See Figure 7 for a typical organization of a retailer's sales promotion division.

## SALES PROMOTION PLANNING

There is now fairly widespread agreement in all levels of the fashion industry that effective sales promotion comes as a result of careful planning. Some firms have developed this procedure to a greater degree than others, especially the giant textile producers, leading apparel manufacturers, and major department stores and chains. Generally, the larger the business and the more people involved in the execution of sales promotion, the greater the need for a structured plan. See Figure 8 for a typical long range sales promotion planning chart for advertising.

This particular chart is designed for the advertising component of the whole sales promotion plan. There would be a display plan, publicity plan and others in addition to such an advertising plan.

### SALES PROMOTION PLAN

The typical *Sales Promotion Plan* contains the following elements.

DEFINITION OF SPECIFIC SALES OBJECTIVES—These could include: a specified increase in sales for a period of time; adding new customers to the firm's active list; promoting certain brands; introducing new services or presenting new fashion trends.

EXPENSE—It is necessary to determine how much money will be needed to cover the expenses of the plan—so that the cost and the resultant benefits can be evaluated.

KEYNOTE—The basic promotional idea(s) or themes for the plan must be created and developed. Often an idea is adapted from past successes of the business—or from traditional events which have proved effective. Whatever is decided, the plan should center on keynotes designed to accomplish the previously stated sales objectives. Every activity planned should support the designated themes and keynotes.

ACTIVITIES—Decision must be made as to which selling activity can best do the job. The combination of the various sales promotion

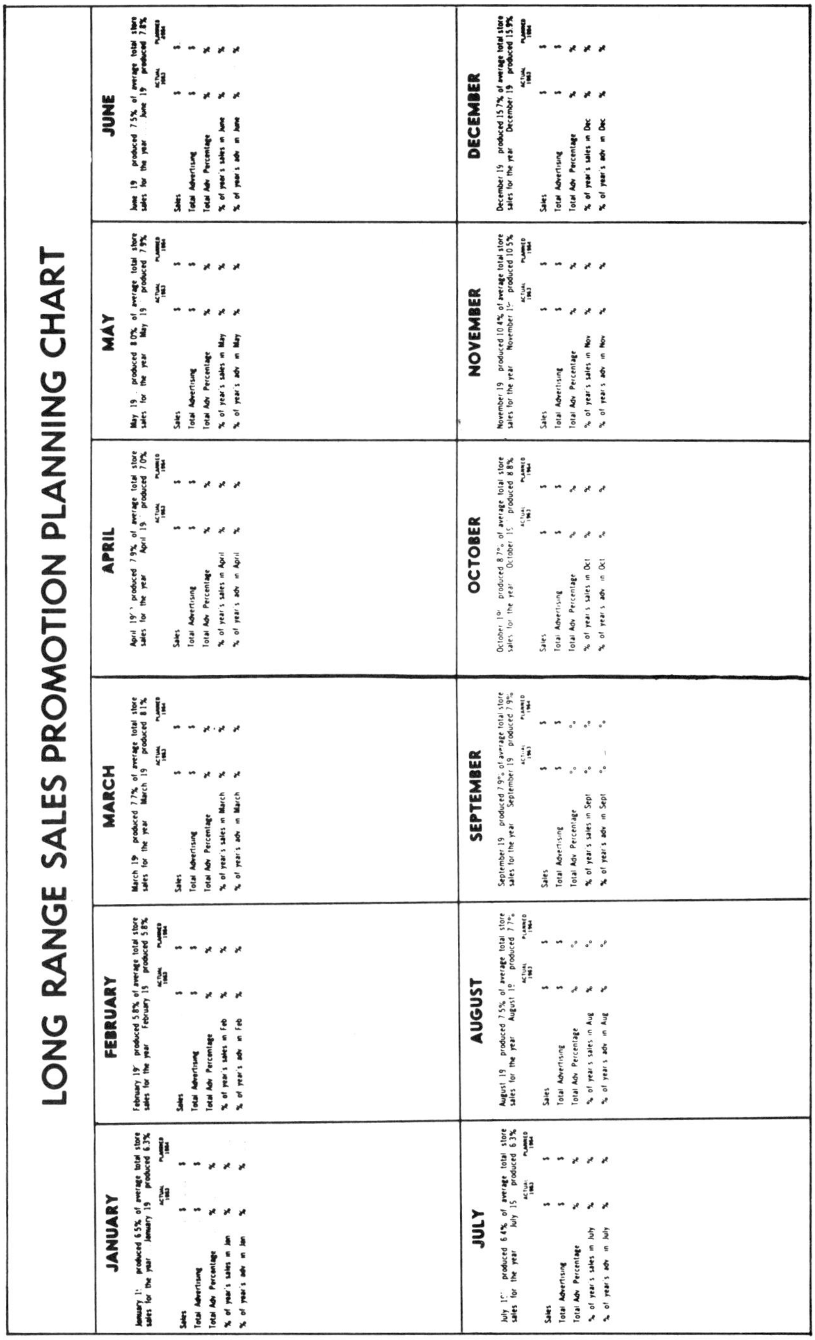

Figure 8. A long range sales promotion planning chart for advertising. (Sales Promotion Calendar from the N.R.M.A.)

activities appropriate to the plan must be outlined and scheduled. The thoughtful coordination of these activities to complement and supplement each other for maximum selling impact is essential.

RESPONSIBILITY—The assignment of responsibility and duty to specific people and departments. Too often a program is outlined and begun with no clear-cut assignment of responsibility. This is a good way *"not* to get off the ground."

EVALUATION—There are methods for testing the effectiveness of promotional activities. These help to guide future efforts. Among these methods are: direct mailing, inquiry, store sales records, use of split runs in newspaper advertising, and other changes in the media mix.

In the next chapter we will show an example of an *advertising planning calendar worksheet* used for scheduling and budgeting advertising.

Any company's sales promotion planning is of paramount concern to all levels and areas of management. A firm must make and sell its products at a profit to stay in business. Selling the company's product is the responsibility of sales management and sales promotion. Developing and producing products which customers want and which can be sold at a competitive price is the responsibility of the management and production divisions of a business. Sales promotion specialists are charged with developing customers and markets where the product can be sold. They must create and execute sales promotion plans which coordinate those sales promotion activities which can best sell the customer—*and help keep him sold.*

Modern marketing concepts call for close cooperation of all the divisions and activities of a business.

In the fashion industry, the manufacturers of raw materials and garments have to sell markets which are more diversified than the local markets of retailers. The manufacturer will be selling customers from many different areas with different requirements. For these reasons many producers retain outside marketing and sales promotion consultants and advertising agencies to work with their own executives in the planning, coordination and implementing of advertising and promotion activities.

Retailers have found it more difficult to work with external advertising agencies, and generally rely upon comprehensive internal departments.

## THE ROLE OF THE ADVERTISING AGENCY

Calling the advertising agency by any other name may not be just as sweet—but it could be more accurate. A more accurate name for this complex business would be *Communications* or *Marketing Communications*. The full service advertising agency is now involved in so many research, marketing, communications, and sales promotion functions that the mere preparation and placement of advertising would severely limit its usefulness to most clients. This is also true in the fashion industry where the agency helps primary raw material producers and secondary apparel manufacturers develop the "right product at the right time at the right price" and helps to create effective channels of distribution in selected markets. Marketing and sales promotion in the full service agency are functions which help a manufacturer stimulate his sales force, design sales presentations, train salespeople, plan sales conventions and exhibits, and organize sales drives. The advertising agency can research markets and also conduct research studies in consumer motivations, preferences, and buying patterns. The agency must be aware of the client's market position, product and institutional objectives, and long range goals. Marketing must be accompanied by comprehensive media research for strategy and planning in media selection. Advertising and direct-mail campaigns, packaging, dealer aids, cooperative advertising, tie-in promotions, and point-of-purchase display materials are planned and produced. These functions are offered by agencies as a full service or a supplement to the firm's own staff. The agency role today is to assist a client in the marketing and communications needed for selling his product. In the full sense of the meaning of marketing this includes product research, market research, developing distribution channels, and any or all of the communications and promotional activities—advertising, display, publicity, personal selling.

The following are the *Service Standards of the American Association of Advertising Agencies (The 4As).* They represent the fundamentals of *full agency service.*

1. *Study of the Product*—The agency studies a client's product or service to determine its market position and researches its

advantages, disadvantages, how it compares with its competitors, its uses, how favorably it is priced, packaging, and availability. Agencies use interviews, questionnaires, field research and all other published information to learn what customers think about a product and its competition.

2. *Present and Potential Market*—A thorough market analysis is conducted for the product—who buys it, or might buy it, when, where, and why. Potential markets are explored to increase market share and revitalize performance.

3. *Factors of Distribution*—How to get the product to the point-of-sale. Who are the key wholesalers or jobbers? The pacesetting retail stores or chains? What pricing structure or promotions would move the product?

4. *Knowledge of Media*—According to the 4As' Service Standards, the agency should have "a knowledge of all available media and means which can profitably be used to carry the interpretation of the product or service to consumer, wholesaler, dealer, contractor or other factor." Media need to be analyzed as to character; influence; the quantity, quality and location of audience or circulation; physical requirements and costs. The agency presents media strategy and media plans to the client which will identify the best potential customers and those media which will get the message to them at the lowest effective cost.

5. *Formulating the Plan*—The plan recommends: markets to be reached; distribution changes, if any; pricing; media channels to consumer and to the trade; copy appeals and approaches; appropriate message for each channel; merchandising factors (salespeople, dealers, distributors) needed; how much should be appropriated for advertising and promotion.

6. *Execution of the Plan*—This involves all of the creative services of copy, layout, art and advertising production for print and broadcast advertising, direct mail, packaging, display, point-of-purchase materials, sales presentations, publicity and press kits. The agency must develop systems for his client to contract for media space and time, billing and paying procedures, distributing produced materials to media, and checking and verifying ads and commercials after they have been run.

7. *Cooperating with Sales Work*—This may be the most descriptive standard of what is meant by a full service agency. Cooperation with the client's sales effort emphasizes that advertising cannot work in a vacuum; it is a link in the marketing process that extends from the producer to the consumer. The agency may also be involved in package design, sales research, sales training, preparation of sales and service literature, designing of merchandising displays, publicity and public relations. The agency's involvement requires strong consumer orientation. The advertiser may know most about his product, but it is the agency's job to know the consumers' wants and needs.

AGENCY COMPENSATION—There are many arrangements which agencies negotiate individually with different clients. The 4As has identified eight principal kinds of overall compensation arrangements between agencies and clients.

1. Media commissions plus charges for materials and services purchased for clients plus charges for some specific inside services.
2. Media commissions plus charges for materials and services purchased, but with no charges for any inside services.
3. Media commissions only.
4. Arrangement 1, 2 or 3 above plus an overall additional fee.
5. Arrangement 1, 2 or 3 above, but with a profit floor and a profit ceiling.
6. A minimum fee, against which media commissions are credited.
7. An overall fee agreed upon in advance.
8. The overall cost of handling the entire account, or cost plus, calculated after the work is done.

Media commissions continue to be the largest ingredient in agency compensation, although their importance varies with the size of the agency. Large agencies with larger accounts using much space and time tend to have more of their income in media commissions, smaller agencies tend more toward fees.

Figure 9 is an organizational plan for a *full service* advertising agency.

Most agencies who work for fashion firms are extremely retail-oriented. They realize the vitality of selling activities which get

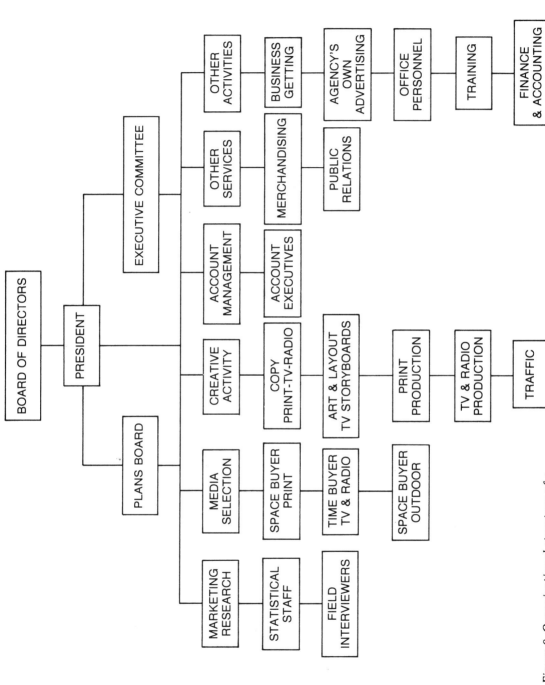

*Figure 9. Organizational structure of a full service advertising agency.*

their inspiration from consumer wants and needs. Those efforts which best supplement personal selling and coordinate sales promotion activities are the basis of agency service. The extent to which the agency gets involved is largely up to the client and his requirements. Many fashion producers (especially the large textile firms and larger apparel manufacturers) have substantial staffs of their own which perform the aforementioned functions.

Agencies have generally found that regardless of how limited their original arrangement is: if they can really help a client, they are gradually asked to do more and more. A good agency is considered a staff element in the organizational structure of many firms in the fashion industry.

We have not mentioned agency service to the retailer—and purposely.

Here the story is quite different. It is difficult for the average agency to provide service for retailers. Agencies which have been most successful serving retail accounts found it necessary to institute specialized "retail" advertising departments which are equipped to handle retail store advertising. These departments are specifically designed to handle daily newspaper advertising with its problems of quick deadlines and last-minute changes.

The advertising agency which equips itself for this service is prepared to plan and produce *all* of a store's advertising. This, however, is not as common as the case of agencies which undertake to work on certain institutional campaigns, to prepare special advertising material and research, and offer counsel on marketing, media planning and copy concepts. By limiting their service, they are not involved with the constant pressure caused by the day-in, day-out advertising and sales promotion in which retail stores must engage.

Several large stores which have their own advertising departments use outside agencies to prepare all of their institutional advertising, while they themselves prepare the product advertising. Other stores may engage an agency to handle their radio and television advertising while handling their newspaper advertising themselves.

The most successful example of a large store/advertising agency relationship has been the inspired collaboration of Ohrbach's in New York City and the agency Doyle, Dane, Bernbach. The institutional advertising produced by this combination not only stimulated

Figure 10. Compare Ohrbach's institutional/product
approach in this coat ad to the Macy's coat ad (Figure 11).

*Figure 11.*

the progress of the store, but is universally regarded as a classic in retail institutional advertising. The use of institutional advertising by retailers is now an established and recognized technique. The pressure of increased competition from innovative, charismatic new retailers has increased the need for "selling the institution" as well as the product. Note Ohrbach's new approach in this recent precedent setting ad which is product *and* institutional and mentions the competition! See Figure 10.

Agencies with producers such as fabric mills and apparel manufacturers as clients are more likely to be engaged in a full range of services and activities described in the 4As Service Standards, which help originate, develop, package, distribute and promote products. They create publicity programs, advise in matters of public relations, and engage in various forms of research. The number of agencies seeking business from fashion producers grows daily. The range of services which agencies render to retailers is much more limited. The problems of handling the sales promotion of retailers inhibit the agency's full-scale entry into retail sales promotion.

# 3

# How Much for Fashion Sales Promotion?

The amount of money which a company spends on all its sales promotion activities is called its sales promotion *appropriation*. This figure (average 1% to 4%), is determined by the firm's financial advisors to top management, who base it on how much the business can (and should) spend on selling activities to maintain and/or *increase* its volume of sales. The general practice is to appropriate for sales promotion, *a fixed percentage of anticipated annual sales*. It is commonly believed in the business community that a business which does not "go ahead" each year is falling behind. Thus, the appropriation for sales promotion is not a percentage of what the company's sales were *last* year. It is rather, what sales volume will result by increasing sales promotion *this year*. The theory is that the added appropriation for promotion will be justified by increased sales volume.

The appropriation is then *allocated* to the various sales promotion activities. Management committees from the merchandising and control divisions work with the sales promotion division to decide what emphasis to put on advertising as compared to display, publicity or fashion shows. The next step is the development of the advertising plan, display plan, publicity plan—each of which is derived from the objectives and keynotes of the sales promotion plan.

Some firms find that their customers can be sold more effectively by allocating most of their appropriation for various types of advertising. Some rely more on publicity. The nature of sales promotion *allocations* is a reflection of the best way to sell the firm's product to its particular *audience* or group of customers. The allocations must be then distributed to the different "avenues" for sales promotion which can carry sales messages. These avenues (newspapers, magazines, direct mail, radio, television) are called *Media*, (*medium* is the singular of media). Figure 12 illustrates a typical sales promotion appropriation with allocations to the separate activities and media.

*Media budgets* are determined by an analysis of which media are most productive in reaching the company's audience. These budgets

*Figure 12. A typical sales promotion appropriation to the separate activities and media.*

ANTICIPATED ANNUAL SALES VOLUME
$1,000,000

APPROPRIATES
2%
OF
A.S.V. FOR
SALES PROMOTION

S.P. APPROPRIATION
IS
$20,000
(2% OF $1 MILLION)
(SALES PROMOTION
PLAN IS DEVELOPED)

10%
FASHION
SHOWS
$2,000

20%
DISPLAY
$4,000

50%
TO
ADVERTISING
$10,000

20%
PUBLICITY
$4,000

ALLOCATIONS

ADVERTISING BUDGET
$10,000
(ADVERTISING PLAN IS
DEVELOPED)
FURTHER BREAKDOWN
INTO
MEDIA BUDGET
$1,000 RADIO
$5,000 NEWSPAPERS
$4,000 DIRECT MAIL

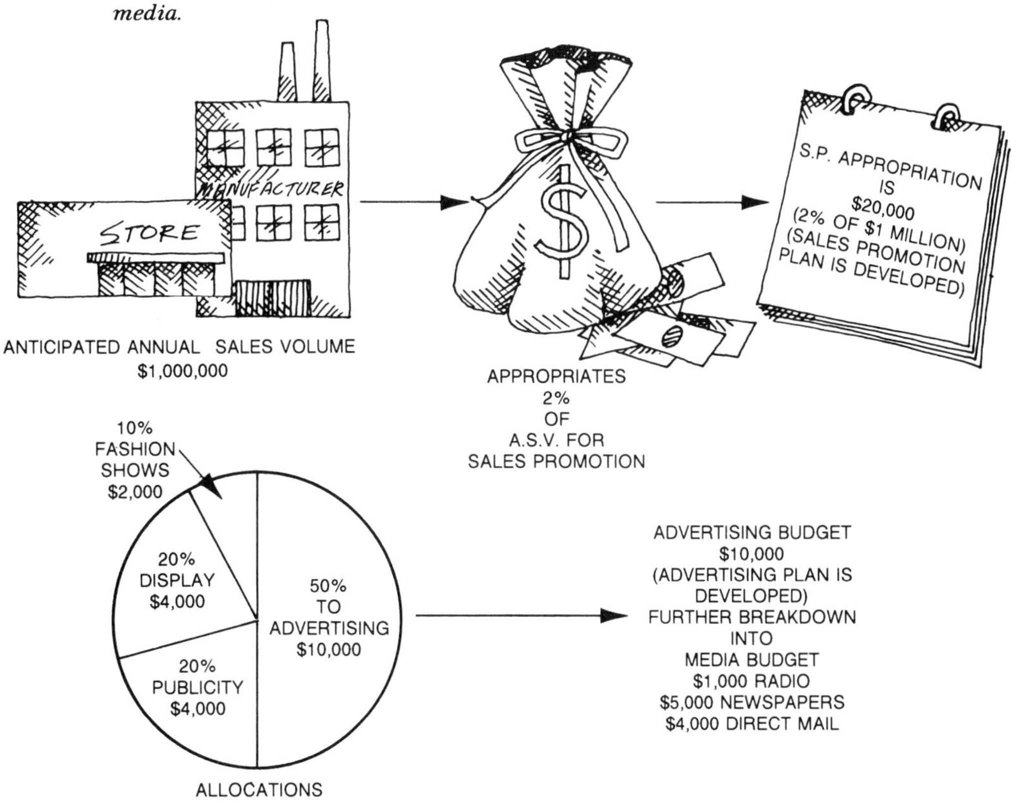

are distributed to product classifications or departments generally on the basis of anticipated sales or profits. A simple example of this might be the allocation of twice as much money from the newspaper advertising budget to the sportswear division in a retail store, than to the sporting goods division. The basis for this distribution might be that the sportswear division *contributes twice as much* to the store's annual sales volume as the sporting goods division. You can see why this should be, if you again consider that the *appropriation* was determined by volume of sales in the first place—*thus, potential volume of sales for a product would be the yardstick for how much you would spend to promote its sale.*

## HOW MUCH FOR RETAIL PROMOTION?

Retailers budget for sales promotion in much the same as they budget for buying merchandise. As we indicated previously, the overall amount which the average retailer appropriates for all activities of promotion is approximately one to four percent of sales. This *appropriation for promotion* is usually prepared for six months to a year and adjusted during a six-month term if circumstances require it.

The size of retail promotional appropriations is dependent upon many factors. It is difficult to describe a typical store when we discuss how much is spent for sales promotion. Each retailer has individual promotional goals and objectives depending upon—how long the store has been established, how well known it is in its trading area, the pattern of its customer traffic, current economic and local conditions, its size, location, its merchandise philosophy and fashion authority, the nature of its competition and the quality of its advertising and promotion efforts, and the costs of newspaper space and of other media in the store's trading area.

Very few retailers can afford to spend more than four percent of their sales for promotion, and many spend only a fraction of four percent. Smaller stores may use little or no advertising, using window and departmental display and direct mail as their methods of communicating with customers.

### PLANNING TO PROMOTE—THE PROMOTION CALENDAR

A Sales Promotion Calendar is a version of the sales promotion plan we discussed previously. It indicates when, what merchandise, which activity, who will develop, and how much is budgeted for promotions. Promotions which are based on traditional seasonal events, Christmas Gifting, January White Sales, August Fur Events, Valentine's Day, Mother's Day, Father's Day, are not difficult to locate in time on the Calendar. The timing of other promotions is not as obvious, and their timing is extremely important to sales success. For example, the promotion of a sale should occur in advance of the event and only during the beginning. Advertising, display and other promotion activities should be planned to break in advance of the maximum sales period in order to stimulate early customer responses for additional sales.

Most experienced advertisers and retail buyers know how useless it is to promote those "buyer's mistakes" which are candidates for markdown. Merchandise which has been initially rejected by customers, or has passed its peak of popularity in customer acceptance should not be featured in advertisements or displays. Merchandise which is most wanted by customers, or new products with current appeal should be selected for advertising and promotion. The planning of sales promotion includes the developing of a long range sales promotion master plan, and separate plans for each of the promotion activities. These plans, often presented in the form of a calendar, are useful tools which aid merchandise managers, buyers and sales promotion departments in coordinating buying, merchandising and promotion for the most effective acceleration of sales. The long range sales promotion planning chart reproduced on page 25, is for a year's *advertising*. It includes the traditional and innovative sales and events which the store advertised the year before. There is a blank space in each time slot to indicate the activities planned for the current year as well as the previous year's volume of sales in dollars, and the dollar sales volume anticipated for this year. This is valuable information for management to consider and compare in their advertising and promotion planning for the next six months to a year.

The planning worksheet (Figure 13) is used by retailers to schedule the store's advertising in newspapers for each month of the year.

Retailers have two sources of advertising and promotion funds, namely the allocation from their own sales promotion appropriation and cooperative advertising allowances received from manufacturers. Sales promotion as an expenditure is quite important to

## 1. SET A SALES GOAL

| DEPT | SALES GOAL | % OF GOAL |
|---|---|---|
| 101 | $ 42,000 | 28 % |
| 102 | 10,500 | 7 % |
| 103 | 18,000 | 12 % |
| 104 | 22,500 | 15 % |
| 105 | 25,500 | 17 % |
| 106 | 15,000 | 10 % |
| 107 | 16,500 | 11 % |
|  | $ _____ | ____ % |
|  | $ _____ | ____ % |
| TOTALS | $ 150,000 | 100 % |

## 2. DECIDE HOW MUCH ADVERTISING

_____ 3 % of sales

_____ $ 4,500 dollars

_____ $ 1.50 / line rate

_____ 3000 lineage

## 3. DECIDE WHAT TO PROMOTE

Write in percents of month's sales which each department contributes. Allot percents of the month's advertising on an equivalent basis. Calculate the lineage for each department.

| DEPT | % OF SALES | % OF ADV. | LINEAGE |
|---|---|---|---|
| 101 | 28 % | 28 % | 840 |
| 102 | 7 % | 7 % | 210 |
| 103 | 12 % | 12 % | 360 |
| 104 | 15 % | 15 % | 450 |
| 105 | 17 % | 17 % | 510 |
| 106 | 10 % | 10 % | 300 |
| 107 | 11 % | 11 % | 330 |
|  | ____ | ____ | ____ |
|  | ____ | ____ | ____ |
| TOTALS | 100% | 100% | 3000 l. |

| SUNDAY | MONDAY | TUESDAY |
|---|---|---|
| **1** Depts. 101=200 l. 104=100 l. [300 lines in ad] Lead Item...price Item...price Item...price Item...price | **2** Men's Nite for Gift Shopping | **3** |
| **8** Depts 105=150 l. 104=150 l. [300 lines in ad] Lead Item...price Item...price Item...price Item...price | **9** Women's Nite for Gift Shopping | **10** |
| **15** Depts 101=220 l. 106=180 l. [400 lines in ad] Lead Item...price Item...price Item...price Item...price | **16** Children's Nite for Gift Shopping | **17** |
| **22** Depts 106=150 l. 107=150 l. [300 lines in ad] Lead Item...price Item...price Item...price Item...price | **23** "Last Minute" Nite for Gift Shopping | **24** |
| **29** End of Mo. Sale Ad Depts 101=200 l. 104=150 l. 102=50 l. [400 lines in ad] Sale Item...price Item...price Item...price | **30** Gift Exchange and Sale Nite | **31** |

| WEDNESDAY | THURSDAY | FRIDAY | SATURDAY |
|---|---|---|---|
| 4<br>"Gift Giving Ideas" Ad<br>All Departments<br>300 lines in ad<br>Lead Item ... price<br>Item ... price<br>Item ... price<br>Item ... price | 5 | 6<br>Special Xmas<br>Night Opening | 7 |
| 11 | 12<br>"Special Days Sale" Ad<br>depts 101 = 150 l.<br>102 = 50 l.<br>104 = 100 l.<br>300 lines in ad<br>Sale Item ... price<br>Item ... price<br>Item ... price | 13<br>Shopping Mall Xmas Days<br>Special Xmas<br>Night Opening | 14 |
| 18 | 19<br>Depts 101 = 270 l.<br>104 = 130 l.<br>400 lines in ad<br>Sale Item ... price<br>Item ... price<br>Item ... price<br>Item ... price | 20<br>Special Xmas<br>Night Opening | 21 |
| 25 | 26<br>Post-Holiday Sale<br>Depts. 103 = 135 l.<br>104 = 145 l.<br>105 = 130 l.<br>400 lines in ad<br>Sale Item ... price<br>Item ... price<br>Item ... price<br>Item ... price | 27 | 28 |
|  |  |  |  |

*Figure 13. An advertising scheduling worksheet such as this is what the average retailer uses to schedule the store's advertising for a month in a systematic plan. It is a guide for buyers and advertising personnel which includes SALES GOALS, AMOUNTS BUDGETED FOR ADVERTISING and WHAT WILL BE ADVERTISED.*

retailers. The average retailer's large expense items are—rent, payroll and sales promotion. Remember too, that advertising and promotion are primarily responsible for generating customer traffic and purchasing which produces the entire sales income of the store.

## HOW THE RETAILER BUDGETS FOR PROMOTION

The retailer makes an attempt to accurately predict his anticipated sales volume—upon which the size of his appropriation for promotion will depend. Certainly this prediction cannot be absolutely on target—the best that the retailer can do is estimate and adjust the promotion expense/sales volume ratio for the six month period.

There are three traditional methods which retailers employ:
1. The "top-to-bottom" method
2. The "bottom-to-top" ("bottom-up") method
3. "All one can afford" method

### TOP-TO-BOTTOM METHOD

The top-to-bottom approach is the method most likely to be used by large retailers. Store management designates goals for sales volume over a six month or year period. The estimates for the various advertising and promotion activities are calculated using the store's predetermined appropriation percentage (approximately 1% to 4%). All of these goals and estimates are developed out of the store's past experience and its need to go ahead each year. The top-to-bottom approach is a natural approach for large, well-established retailers whose sales volume has reflected a steady growth through the year.

Once the total appropriation for all promotion has been determined, the next step is to allocate (or divide) this expense amount among the various activities of sales promotion. The illustration on page 35 is a graphic example of appropriation and allocation breakdowns by percentages. For example, an advertising allocation is then divided into media budgets—newspaper advertising, radio and television, direct mail. The next step is to allocate shares of these funds to store merchandise divisions and departments. The method is similarly applied for display, publicity and other promotion activities.

The top-to-bottom method allows top management to exercise

tight control of promotion expenses compared to sales volume. But this method may not always reflect the knowledge of and feeling for promotional opportunities for sales volume which merchandise managers and their buyers have. Adjustments can be effected by changing percentage ratios designated to specific merchandise divisions and departments.

## BOTTOM-TO-TOP METHOD

Bottom-to-top budgeting attempts to overcome the flaw mentioned above by allowing specific merchandise divisions or departments who are responsible for sales to plan promotion expenditures. The philosophy here is that merchandise managers and buyers are closer to consumer buying behavior and merchandise acceptance than top store management is, and consequently are better equipped to estimate sales goals.

Bottom-to-top budgeting for promotion is done divisionally or departmentally, producing estimates on a day-to-day, week-to-week basis. Merchandise managers and their buyers may calculate the number of lines of newspaper advertising space they will need for a prescribed period. This results in a newspaper advertising schedule and an advertising budget for the period.

It is easy to see why this is not a widely used method. Store management in most large stores are not likely to give up their centralized control of sales promotion expenditures.

## ALL ONE CAN AFFORD METHOD

The previously discussed methods (particularly the top-to-bottom) are easily the most likely used by retailers. The traditional predictability of consumer demand and buyer behavior seem to work well for the use of these methods. The unpredictable, however, seems to be more and more a factor in our uncertain economy, and stores are now more often faced with fluctuating demand and sales volume. Very strong competitive pressures from retail innovators plus the changing practices of the manufacturers of fashion merchandise are now compelling retailers to re-evaluate their estimates of sales periodically.

The established retailer is increasingly confronted by competitors who open new stores or present new services for customers. "Meeting the competition" is the most likely reason for a retailer to use the "all one can afford" method of budgeting for promotion.

Advertising and promotion are certainly not exclusive to large retailers. It has been estimated that over 75 percent of all medium-sized and small retailers spend money on advertising and promotion. Certainly these "appropriations" hardly compare with large retailers. The small retailer, however, may make a substantial effort in planning and producing advertising, display and publicity. Planning methods in small stores vary greatly—mainly in that the planning periods are not as long range. The small or medium size retailer relies on a combination of methods (possibly *all* of the above three) to determine how much to spend on advertising and promotion.

It would be foolhardy and irresponsible for anyone to try to present principles on how much to spend on sales promotion in order to solve *any* problem in fashion selling. Each firm on every level of the fashion industry (primary, secondary and retail) has individual sales objectives which are relevant to its products, its policies and its customers. Each producer, from raw materials to finished apparel, must also be a seller who knows the wants and needs of his customers. As a seller, he tries to design a sales promotion program which will present his story most effectively to the buyer of his product.

The firm's particular financial structure, fiscal policies, and profit margin will determine how much it can spend on sales promotion. It would be prudent here to consult with controllers and accountants. The designing of messages, appeals and approaches, and where to place emphasis on products and institution, is a job for marketing, merchandising and promotion practitioners.

The planning of a sales promotion program involves the selection and coordination of activities which can do the best job of selling products and ideas. Most of the following chapters of this book deal with the purposes of the various advertising and promotion activities, their individual characteristics, and some general procedures used in their application.

# 4

# Advertising
# To Promote Fashion

Advertising has become as much a part of people's lives as their daily newspapers. The student comes to a study of this promotion activity with many preconceived notions and pronounced points of view. This recognized familiarity is actually familiarity with the "end product" of advertising, the advertisement. This knowledge does not always include an *understanding* of the role advertising plays in the economic process of this nation. Those who condemn or praise advertising without qualification are in a sense condemning or praising our whole economic system of which advertising is a very obvious part.

There has been a tendency to degrade the business of advertising. A common expression is the reference to those engaged in the business as "the Madison Avenue boys." Justification for such references is that advertising is "sneaky," and that it contains "hidden persuasion" or "subliminal seduction" designed to influence people to buy the things they do not need or want.

While it is true that advertising whets appetites when it is well written; that advertising informs the public of what is available and where it can be found, it is not true that advertising *forces* the sale of unwanted merchandise. Quite the contrary, one cardinal rule advertisers have learned is that it is wasteful to spend advertising dollars on merchandise unwanted in the marketplace. There is solid evidence that huge advertising expenditures and vigorous promotion do not guarantee success. For example, Ford's short-lived Edsel car; the shift dress silhouette; and the midi length—all heavily promoted some years ago are part of a long list of flops.

Advertising is a social as well as an economic force. Firms that produce and sell goods use advertising to help introduce and to sell those goods. The public enjoys those products, or benefits by them, or the advertising will soon fail. Advertising does *not* sell merchandise. It informs and can *influence* selling of goods, services and institutions. This action then provides the economy with not only goods and services, but also with jobs. In the final essence, however, the consumer makes the decision for success or failure.

Advertising grew up with America. In order to succeed in business some years ago, a man thought advertising was the sure road to wealth. Just as America is now involved in the science of the computer, advertising is moving into a highly technological era. Test markets are used for test advertising along with scientific research methods. The advertiser with the big budget spends a considerable percentage of his investment in test programs to determine the strongest and most effective way to spend his advertising dollars. Guesswork can be very costly and ineffective.

Even the company with the small budget does well to engage professional talent in determining what constitutes good advertising and the best medium to use to reach the most responsive audience for its product.

In this chapter, it is intended that some of the fundamentals of advertising be clarified, and that some of the mystery and misconceptions be eliminated, not just for those who may be interested in a career in advertising and promotion, but for anyone who will have an interest in the subject or will be called upon to make communications decisions in the fashion business.

Also in this chapter, we are concerned with the role that fashion advertising plays in the sales promotion of fashion. "Fashion advertising" is no different from "non-fashion advertising." What is different are the buying motivations. Each product, apparel or otherwise, has its own appeals and motivations to buy—yet they do have some common denominators. These are the similarities in the needs and wants of people. The advertising of fashion is keyed to the motivations of customers on each of the market levels. In our growing economy, these customers, both trade and consumer, are too numerous, too widely scattered, or too inaccessible to be influenced adequately by *personal selling* at the point-of-sale. This is why advertising becomes an indispensable part of the sales promotion effort. It is a form of mass communication which was developed because sellers needed a way of getting a sales message to customers away from the point-of-sale. This message is intended to bring customers to the point-of-sale, ready to be "sold."

A formal definition of advertising would be: A nonpersonal method of influencing sales by sending a sponsored and paid message through mass media to a mass audience of potential customers.

In the next chapter we will discuss mass media for fashion advertising, and how fashion firms use media to communicate with customers.

## GENERAL OPERATING PROCEDURE

The organization of the advertising effort on different levels of the fashion business varies. The following procedure, however, is common to any business in the conduct of their advertising effort.

1. The advertising program has to be planned with the policies and objectives of management in mind.
2. What to advertise is determined by those closest to the needs and wants of the company's customers. The selection of products and ideas which will result in the most profitable business for the firm is the responsibility of merchandising and sales executives.
3. The coordination of advertising activities, media planning and selection, scheduling and production are the responsibility of the advertising manager under the supervision of the marketing director and/or the sales promotion manager.

Planning committees for advertising will include representatives from all areas: management, marketing, sales, merchandising and sales promotion. Decisions on policy, objectives, themes, media and budget are a result of the application of their knowledge and experience.

*Figure 14.*

**Chalk up a few more reasons for living in Jones, New York.**

Each of the five easy pieces we show counts as one. To add to the list, this is navy and white chalk striping. And navy is back in a big way. The fit you've always loved about Jones, New York is back to. But we think you'll find the softened shapes a delightful addition.

From the left: The big, blousy sweater in ecru wool. S, M or L sizes, 38.00   To match with the navy chalks in a fine wool blended with a touch of polyester Pleated Trousers, 52.00 Unconstructed Shirt-tail Jacket, 76.00 Side-wrap Skirt, 50.00 Diamond foulard on navy ground stock tie: shirt in polyester, 36.00 All for 6 to 14 sizes. **Rena Rowan**. Here in person today when we present the collection with informal modeling from 12:00 to 3:00 Miss Bonwit Sportswear, Eighth Floor, Fifth Avenue at 56th Street, New York

NON-CHALANCE SUITS BONWIT TELLER

*Figures 14 and 15. Compare the two retail ads. What are their objectives? Which is the product ad? The institutional ad? Are either of these ads product/institutional or institutional/product ads?*

*Figure 15.*

FOCUS ON
JONES
NEW YORK

At Gimbels Broadway
at 33rd Street...
Today, September 9th
12:00 to 2:00 pm:
meet our special Jones
New York representative,
**Susan Bissu** who will
be here to present
the new Jones
New York fashions
...soft-tailored
separates that are
right ...in style, in
color, in feel. It all
adds up to you
looking absolutely
fantastic!

FOCUS ON
FABULOUS
EVENTS

At Gimbels Broadway
at 33rd Street...
12:30 to 2:30 pm:
Today, September 9th
Focus on fitness
for fashion and
meet the experts...
**Lori Stevens**,
noted diet/nutrition
authority, who will talk on
health and fitness
...then watch modern
jazz instructor,
**David Harris** of
Ballet Arts and his
Dancers demonstrate
jazz exercises.
You'll meet **Serena** who
will perform and
teach the
fascinating art of
bellydancing.

*Focus on* GIMBELS

focusing on you...and your sense of
individuality. Soft-to-the-touch wool separates
that say you're totally at ease, in fashion,
in life. Focus on Jones New York: easy assemblages
in creamy rich textures. The gray Scottish-check
blazer, $100; the plaid knit vest, navy-burgundy, $33;
the grey polyester crepe de chine stock-tie
blouse, $30; the grey Scottish-check dirndl skirt, $54
Sizes 6 to 14. Signature Sportswear

## TYPES OF ADVERTISING

Advertising can best be classified by the sales objectives which it hopes to attain. An advertisement in any medium is designed to sell either a product(s) or the company (institution) behind the product. The two broad classifications of advertising are called *product* and *institutional.*

### PRODUCT ADVERTISING

*Product* advertising is designed to sell products. Its primary objective is the *immediate* sale of merchandise. Product ads will include *identification, description* and *price* of featured products so that customers can make various decisions before they arrive at the point-of-sale. A product advertisement can pre-sell merchandise or bring customers to a point-of-sale where personal selling takes over to complete the sale (see Figure 14).

### INSTITUTIONAL ADVERTISING

*Institutional* advertising is designed to build a reputation for a firm. Its primary objective is to keep customers sold over a *long period of time.* Institutional ads promote the policies, facilities, merchandise, departments, features, services and/or personnel of a business. The purpose is to seek the steady patronage of customers by convincing them of the firm's prominence and the benefits that it offers (see Figure 15).

All levels of the fashion industry use product and institutional advertising. We will examine next, the *newspaper* advertising of a department store to indicate the different types of product and institutional advertisements used to attain *immediate* and *longer range* sales objectives.

## REPRESENTATIVE TYPES OF RETAIL PRODUCT ADVERTISEMENTS

### SINGLE ITEM ADVERTISEMENTS

*Single item* advertisements, usually 2 or 3 columns wide, feature a single style which may be a best-seller or is fast becoming a most-wanted item in demand at the time. Figure 16 is a reproduction of an ad for the classic "model's coat." The merchandise in this case

Even if you've
never before felt
model perfect in the
morning, you can look it!

In our crisp Model's Coat.
A play of fresh stripes
on chambray. With an easy
button front and softly
tucked yoke. Polyester and
cotton chambray for P, S, M
or L sizes, 20.00
Robes, Fifth Floor

BONWIT
TELLER

*Figure 16. A typical single item advertisement for a perennial best seller.*

*Figure 17.*
*An assortment ad*
*presents the depth*
*and breadth of*
*merchandise offered*
*in a store.*

# Now you get wonderful <u>savings</u> on fine Leather Handbags Sale 22.90 to 49.90

**Now's the time to find
your Fall bag in our
great collection,
at the prices that
please you most.**

We've only sketched
a few from our big,
beautiful collection.
Leathers at 22.90, more
still at 29.90 and 39.90,
and leather luxuries at 49.90.
All bags are specially
purchased or reduced
from stock. Come see
all the handsome shapes,
the fall colors, the
luxury details. And every
bag in this great group
is fine leather. So
come in today for your
favorites. Remember,
the early bird
gets the best choice.
Handbags, main floor,
Fifth Avenue, and
branches. Sorry,
no mail or phone.

B. Altman & Co

50

is illustrated, identified by style designation or label, described, and priced.

## ASSORTMENT ADVERTISEMENTS

An *assortment* advertisement is usually a larger ad than the single item. It features a range of merchandise from a department or division, such as these leather handbags in the ad reproduced in Figure 17. The copy in an assortment ad indicates assortment of styles, color, materials, sizes and range of prices. It can be designed to impress customers with the size and completeness of a department's stock of merchandise.

*Figure 18. The excitement is apparent. This ad introduces themes based upon current customer life styles and special interests.*

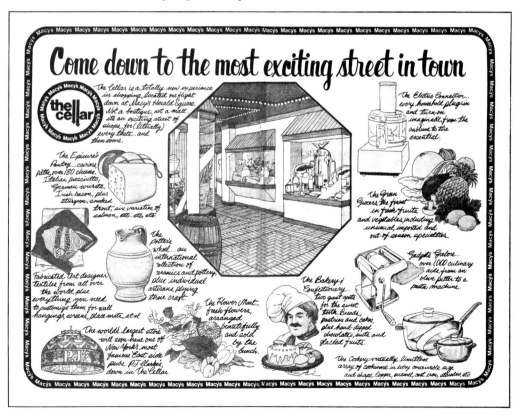

### THEME ADVERTISEMENTS

The *theme* advertisement presents groups of products from various departments, divisions or storewide which have been related by a specific theme. The themes can include a special event (100th Anniversary Sale, Import Festival or as in the ad in Figure 18, a kick-off for "The Cellar," a new department in Macy's, New York, which features home fashions); seasonal promotions (Back-to-School, Christmas gifting); traditional events (January White Sales, August Fur Sales); or current life-style fashion trends.

### DEPARTMENTALIZED OR OMNIBUS ADVERTISEMENTS

In a *departmentalized* or *omnibus* advertisement, many different items related or unrelated, are arranged in graphically separated sections of a large ad to show customers the wide range of merchandise classifications offered by the store. Such an ad may group many items of the most wanted merchandise into one "marketplace." The advertisement offers something to interest and appeal to different readers—a variety of product information based upon their individual wants and needs.

Merchandise which warrants only the expense of small space can be incorporated into the departmentalized or omnibus advertisement. This offers the small space a better chance of being noticed as part of a large space. A variation of the departmentalized advertisement is to group several single item ads together on a page. This can also result in dominating the page and better attention for each small ad. Another technique places a series of single item ads on successive pages for the value of repeated impressions. Figure 19 is a typical departmentalized advertisement.

# PRODUCT ADS CLASSIFIED BY THE CONDITIONS OF SALE

Product advertisements may also be classified by the conditions of sale. Any of the previous classifications—single item, assortment, theme, departmentalized or omnibus—could also be classified as follows.

### REGULAR PRICE

In a *regular price* product ad desirable merchandise is presented for

*Figure 19.*
*Page dominance*
*is obtained in a*
*departmentalized*
*(omnibus) ad by*
*grouping a variety*
*of separate ads*
*into one large ad.*

# Sales! Just-in-time for Fall, 1/3 off corduroy coordinates at Altman's

**Blazer, now 29.90** was 45.00. **Pants, now 14.90,** were 23.00. **Skirt** (not shown), **now 16.90** was 26.00. All, cotton corduroy. **Plaid shirt** in polyester/cotton, **now 11.90,** was 18.00. Sizes 8 to 16. **Turtleneck, now 7.90,** was 12.00, sizes s,m,l. Everything in green or brown. Everything by White Stag. 1/3 off this season's prices. Active Sportswear, third floor, Fifth Avenue and a selection at branches. Sorry, no mail or phone.

**And more fashion savings!**

**Pull-on-skirt, special purchase 10.90.** Self belt, elastic waist. Acrylic knit in basic dark tones. 8 to 18. **Turtleneck, 8.90** was 13.00. Acrylic knit in Fall colors. Back zipper. S,m,l. Sportswear One, main floor, Fifth Avenue, (212) MU9-7000 and a selection at branches.

**And still more savings!**

**Four-gore belted skirt,** not shown, **17.90** was 26.00. Wool/nylon blend in black. 100% wool in gray, taupe, or brown. Sizes 8 to 18. By Century. Moderate Sportswear, sixth floor, Fifth Avenue, (212) MU9-7000 and selection at branches.

## Save on Altman's own hosiery and pantyhose

**Pantyhose**

**Demi-toe now 3/4.00** reg. 1.75 pr. Nylon brief panty, beige, tan, taupe, coffee. Sizes A/B(4'11"-5'5", 90-130 lbs.) C/D(5'5"-5'10", 125-150 lbs.)

**Sheer to the waist sandalfoot now 3/4.00** reg. 1.75 pr. Nylon. Beige, tan, taupe, coffee, navy, off black. Sizes A/B(4'11-5'5") 90-130 lbs. C/D(5'5"-5'10", 125-150 lbs.)

**Queen size demi toe now 3/4.50** reg. 2.00 each. Nylon. Beige, tan, taupe. (1-2x) up to 185 lbs.

**Control top sandalfoot now 3/6.00** reg. 2.50 pr. Lycra® spandex/nylon. Nude, beige, taupe, coffee, off black. A-Small, B-Med., C-Tall, D. Med. tall.

**Support demi-toe now 3/9.00** reg. 3.95 pr. Nude, beige, taupe, Lycra® spandex/nylon. A(Petite) B(Average) C(Med. tall) D(Tall.)

All at Fifth Avenue, (212) MU9-7000 and a selection at branches. These are selected items reduced from stock. Not every item in every color or size. All sales off regular prices end Monday, October 11th. Mail and phone for 10.00 and more, except where otherwise indicated.

**Hosiery:**

**Cantrece® nylon sandalfoot 6/7.50** reg. 1.50 pr. Nude, beige, taupe. A(8½-9½ Med.) B(10-11 Med.)

**Nylon knee highs now 6/3.50,** reg.1.00 ea. Sheer demi-toe sandalfoot or sheer ankle-hi sandalfoot. Beige, taupe, nude, coffee, black, navy. Sizes 8-11. Queen Hi demi toe in black, brown, beige. Sizes 9-12. Opaque demi-toe in navy, berry, rust or gray. (8-11). Hosiery, main floor, Fifth Avenue and branches.

**Designer scarves Now 2/9.00, 4.90 ea.** were 8.00 and 10.00. Paisleys, stripes, geometrics. 24", 28", 30" squares, oblongs. Silk/rayon or polyester. Sorry, no mail or phone. Scarves, main floor, Fifth Avenue, selection at branches.

**Suede gloves now 9.90** were 13.00. Warm acrylic polyester pile lining keeps you warm. Camel, brown or black suede. S(6-6½) M(7) L(7½-8).

**Leather gloves now 12.90** were 17.00. From Italy, pull-on length, silk lined metis leather. Hand-felled hem. Black or brown. Sizes 6½-8. Gloves, main floor, Fifth Avenue and branches.

B. Altman & Co

immediate sale. Its purpose, other than to generate traffic, is to keep customers advised that this store has the fashion they most want at prices which they prefer to pay. The advertisement in Figure 20 is a good example, featuring corduroy coordinates—an important look for the coming season.

*Figure 20.*
*Regular-price*
*advertising to*
*introduce*
*most-wanted*
*fashion.*

**C**orduroy: a new dimension in softness. Rich. Plush. In a velvety pinwale of 100% cotton. A casual elegance in gently tailored shapes. The short, tab-waist baseball jacket with wide collar and cuffs, **70.00,** layered with the newsy cowl-neck sweater, **30.00.** The zip-front pant in the same pale-camel, **41.00.** All three pieces from **Breckenridge.** Sizes 6-14.
Sportswear 70's, Coordinates (89).
Order by mail or dial toll-free
1-800-252-9174.

**The Broadway**

Shop weekdays and Saturday from 10 a.m. and all weekday evenings. ·All stores open Sundays. Order board open 24 hours a day. Dial 1-800-252-9174.

## SPECIAL PRICE

A *special price* type of product ad can be presented as a sale. It seeks immediate response through the appeal of a special price offering. It is usually a result of a special purchase made by the buyer at an off-price. The savings are passed on to the customer. It can also involve a temporary markdown or reduction taken on certain merchandise from a department's stock such as in the ad reproduced in Figure 21.

## CLEARANCE AND REDUCED PRICE

*Clearance* and *reduced price* promotions are necessary to dispose of slow-selling merchandise which may have been already marked down, odd sizes and broken lots. These ads are generally designed

*Figure 22.*
*This ad is designed*
*to appeal to the*
*price-conscious*
*customer who*
*enjoys a bargain*
*from a favorite*
*store.*

56

*Figure 23. Is there any question not answered in this mail-order ad? Would salespeople offer as much information?*

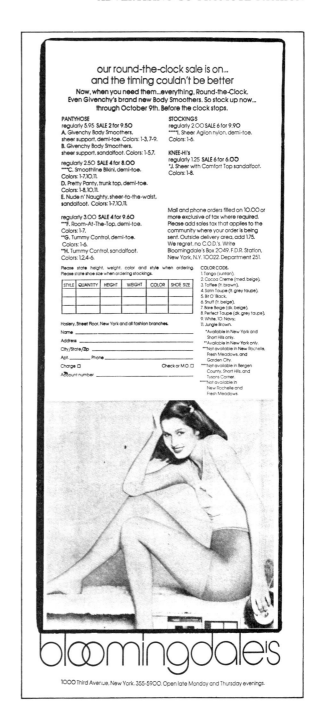

to appeal to regular customers who appreciate a bargain and should be used only when the inventory of merchandise can "back-up the ad." The ad in Figure 22 offers across-the-board price reductions in a clearance of drapery ensembles at "Savings of 20% to 25%."

## MAIL ORDER

The term *mail order* should not be confused with the term *direct mail.* Direct mail is an advertising medium. Any kind of advertising which will allow the customer to place an order by mail or *phone* (which is also considered a "mail order") is considered mail order advertising. Advertising which allows for mail orders could utilize a variety of media as well as direct mail, such as newspapers, magazines, radio, television or even transit advertising. Figure 23 is an example of retail mail-order advertising in a newspaper.

# REPRESENTATIVE TYPES OF RETAIL INSTITUTIONAL ADVERTISING IN NEWSPAPERS AND MAGAZINES

## POLICY

Purpose is to point out to customers what the store stands for in terms of customer's needs and preferences. For example, type of merchandise, conditions of sales, pricing, returns and exchanges, responsibility.

## STORE SERVICES

Conveniences to make shopping pleasant and easier (e.g., delivery, charge accounts, gift wrapping, air conditioning, cafeteria).

## PRESTIGE

A store will advertise to establish or maintain its reputation as a fashion authority, its alertness in introducing new fashion and its exclusiveness. Or it may stress its wide and complete assortments of currently popular fashion and staple merchandise. These ads are often placed in magazines (see Figure 24) and feature fashions from certain departments. Their primary purpose, however, is part of a long range effort to build and to maintain the customer's confidence in the store.

*Figure 24. An institutional ad designed to enhance a retailer's "image" or prestige may actually feature a product. These are often placed in a magazine such as this Lord & Taylor ad in VOGUE Magazine.*

59

*Figure 25. An institutional ad sponsored by an apparel manufacturer to develop recognition of his brand name.*

*Figure 26. A primary producer will run ads to the trade to sell his products to secondary manufacturers of apparel, such as this Burlington Industries ad in WWD.*

## MANUFACTURER INSTITUTIONAL AND PRODUCT ADVERTISING

Manufacturers also have both product and institutional objectives for their advertising. They are involved in selling their institutions as well as the products they manufacture. Much of their product advertising involves the promotion of *brand names*. The purpose of such brand designations is to differentiate their products in the minds of trade customers (professional buyers) and of the ultimate consumer. A dress manufacturer, for example, might run ads in trade publications to convince store buyers that his particular line of *brand-name* dresses for fall constitutes excellent translations of current fashion, offers good quality at a competitive price and would sell well in their stores. Or he might use direct mail to send a similar message. This producer would also be using institutional ads to enhance his reputation for originality, dependability and service.

His advertising program does not stop here. A brand-name manufacturer can also suggest to the ultimate consumer that he recognize, look for and prefer his brand to others.* (See Figure 25.) Here, too, product ads in consumer publications such as *Vogue, Glamour, Mademoiselle, Gentleman's Quarterly,* and *Seventeen,* will present representative items from his current line of products which consumers can purchase at his dealer stores. Institutional ads to the consumer stress the maker's reputation for original design; quality of workmanship; appropriateness of fabric, color and sizes.

The primary producer of raw material for fashion will include product and institutional advertising in his program to sell his firm and its products to apparel manufacturers (Figure 26). These trade advertisements will appear in trade publications. He will address the ultimate consumer in consumer media (national magazines, television) attempting to persuade through his national advertising that fashion products made from his primary product are more desirable (Figure 27).

*Figure 27. National advertising by primary producers is designed to remind consumers to look for a "product made with a product."*

---

*A manufacturer of "unbranded lines" is not interested in identifying his label to consumers. His merchandise is often sold under the store's label.

## CHARACTERISTICS OF AN EFFECTIVE ADVERTISEMENT

How does one evaluate an advertisement? An alert executive ponders this question when he finds that he is responsible to approve or disapprove the advertising for his company. There are many factors which could be used in measurement of effectiveness of advertising. Researchers have also developed many methods of measurement. Some of these factors are included in this chapter. Most important, however, is the fact that advertising should not be judged exclusively on the basis of what suits your own tastes.

It must be remembered that advertising is rarely directed to the attention of one person who happens to agree with you and with what you like. If this were so, then the fashion industry would have a far less complicated problem in the selection of merchandise. Every dress department might have all simple classic dresses, or possibly all very fussy types; and every men's clothing department could do well with but one general type of clothes for all men. And so it is true of advertising that it must have appeal for specific market segments or groups of readers, listeners, or viewers, many of whom might just happen not to have your special tastes.

An experienced advertising practitioner should have this ability to prepare ads for selective audiences. It is easy to understand therefore why an exclusive jewelry shop does not use layout, art and copy similar to that of a credit jewelry chain which emphasizes price in its advertising. This does not mean that one must be schooled formally in advertising to be a competent judge. The point is that one must be objective in evaluation of ads. Take into account the medium, the intended audience, the product or service involved, the objectives of the company and of the specific ad. Then, and only then, can one truly and competently judge advertising.

"I like it because I like it" or "I just don't like it" are not logical bases for decisions in advertising.

What makes advertising effective? Will this ad sell? If it were possible for anyone to answer with a high degree of accuracy, the question of whether a specific ad would be successful in the marketplace, this person could make a fortune! This expert would enable advertisers to eliminate costly market research and pre-publication/post-publication copy-testing. Our expert could look at different versions of an ad or campaigns of ads and render his decision.

Of course this is no more possible than accurately predicting whether a song or play will be a hit before its release. For even though professionals with much experience create what they believe will be effective—in the actual performance or at the point-of-sale, it is the consumer public who decides.

One proven technique we can use in judging the effectiveness of advertising is to recognize which *characteristics* are common to successful advertisements.

1. *The main idea is not hidden*—The reader, viewer or listener is left with an impression which he can recall and which adds to the personality and image of the advertiser.

2. *What is the sales objective?*—Is it product or institutional? Why was this ad created? What was the advertiser trying to convey? If this is hard to tell, the ad cannot be very effective.

3. *Continuity*—Advertising should build upon itself. Each advertisement should benefit from the impact of its predecessor —and do the same for its successor.

4. *Identity*—Recognition from consistent style: Layout, typography, copy style, decorative elements, art. Some ads can be identified before a single word of copy is read. Can you identify the ad shown in Figure 28? See if you can isolate the elements which contribute to positive identification.

5. *Relationship between visual and verbal*—The visual part of an advertisement or commercial must be related to the verbal part. As in a good popular song, words and music must help each other. The copy in a print advertisement is visualized by art. In a radio commercial, words are visualized by sound effects and music. In a television commercial, the audio reinforces the video.

6. *Simplicity*—When we add the superfluous we destroy clarity and belief. Shakespeare's ". . . methinks the prisoner doth protest his innocence too much . . ." fits here. Redundancy and irritating repetitions have a place in some types of advertising but today's most sophisticated advertising tries to be concise and direct. This does not inhibit individual style. It rather encourages an approach to style which relies on "nuts and bolts" instead of "false whiskers."

Study the ad in Figure 29. It is an example of a long-running fashion advertising campaign. Evaluate its effectiveness considering the preceding list of characteristics.

# 5

# Motivating Customers through Fashion Appeals

The term *motivation* has been used in the behavioral sciences to describe a *reason why a person will act or behave* in a certain manner. Certain wants or needs will motivate people to act as they do. Sellers are interested in why customers *act* as they do and primarily why they *buy* as they do. The seller is interested in *what motivates the customer to buy.* In order to present customers with powerful incentives to buy, it is necessary to analyze their *needs* and *wants.* Customer motivations differ at different marketing levels, however.

It is important to consider what needs and wants mean to the seller. Customers respond in their buying behavior to needs, wants, attitudes, habits and customs. For our purposes, we shall refer to any need, want, habit or attitude as a motivation. A need is an absence of something which a customer must have, because he finds it essentially useful or desirable. He *needs* this something he lacks and *wants* something that will fill the void. *The seller cannot create the need,* but he can make a customer more conscious of a need and influence him to want certain products to satisfy this need. No list of customer needs or wants could be presented which is totally accurate or complete. The behavior of individuals varies tremendously. Each customer may have different motives from time to time. (Note that we are using the term "customer" to describe any buyer of fashion. The "consumer" is the *ultimate* buyer and user. A sportswear manufacturer's "customer," for example, could be a store buyer.) The motivations of a purchasing agent for a garment producer are different from those of a purchaser for a raw materials producer—and vastly different from the motivations of the ultimate consumer of the product. The first two are buying for their firms, while the consumer is buying for himself. Would this affect individual motivation? The seller must base his reasons to buy on what he feels will motivate his customers. He will be involved with several important questions relating to the customer's buying behavior.

The seller must realize:

1. There are *rational* (e.g., practical considerations such as economy, dependability, service) as well as *emotional* motives (comfort, security, love or prestige) for buying behavior.

*Figure 28. Some ads can be identified even before a single word of copy is read. This ad has a visual and verbal approach which is purely its own. What are the characteristics which give it IDENTITY?*

65

    2. More than one motive, sometimes many motives, can be involved in each purchase, with perhaps one or several of more importance than others.

The seller must also ask the following:

    1. Why do customers *decide to* buy a product?

    2. Why does a customer select one *brand* or type of product?

    3. Why does a customer select one *dealer* over another?

Motivations to buy can be classified into three groups which correspond to these three questions.

PRIMARY MOTIVES—Involve reasons why a customer decides to buy.

SELECTIVE MOTIVES—Influence what type or brand of product a customer will buy.

PATRONAGE MOTIVES—Determine where or from whom a customer will buy.

What are the implications for marketers of fashion in this discussion of customer and consumer behavior? For one thing, consumers' attitudes regarding the value of the fashion product are changing rapidly. Today's consumer is very often hunting for fashion with which to impress himself rather than his sweetheart, his boss, or his "world." These attitudes have developed as our values have changed enough to liberate the average person from traditional cultural and social restraints. Today's consumer is more conscious of his own identity and individuality—he enjoys freedom of choice as never before. Recognizing this, he searches for fashions which more nearly fit his own needs and wants, rather than those of the idealized people in advertisements and commercials.

    Motivational researchers today have to concentrate as much on the response to the medium and message as to response to the product itself. Many advertisements have contained appeals which were in such poor taste as to cause an audience not only to reject the message, but also to mentally boycott the advertiser's family of products.

    The consumer's search for identity is the basic motivational force behind much of fashion sales promotion today. Fashion is no longer limited to the affluent society and the celebrities of New York, Hollywood and Palm Beach. There are women in Albuquerque, New Mexico, and Ames, Iowa, who are as much a part of the vast fashion market as any of the "elegants" portrayed in the pages of *Vogue* and *Women's Wear Daily (WWD)*.

The designers as well as the promoters of fashion would do well to think now of the vast fashion market in terms of individuals, not masses. There are many selective markets for the fashion product, each of which includes people with unique motivational structures and consumer behavior patterns. There are lucrative markets for fashion emerging all over the world which justify their own special sales promotion campaigns from both the producers and the retailers of fashion.

Among all of the promoters and sellers of fashion, the *retailers* of fashion—store presidents, merchandise managers, buyers and salespeople, as well as sales promotion directors and various promotion specialists—have to work most effectively as a team to motivate consumers to buy. Merchandising communications are only as good as the information and meanings they convey accurately. Retailers must design advertising and promotion messages based upon their firsthand knowledge of consumer motivations and satisfactions. The retailer is in a unique position to know consumer feelings about fashion products and the satisfactions desired from them.

Promotional activities which are designed to motivate consumers to make a buying decision should include helpful information as well as persuasion. Today's consumer demands more accurate and realistic information about the features, construction, and performance of fashion products than ever before. They also want to be informed about community and store services, special showings, openings and hours, store consultants, special events, and exhibits. The newspaper advertising of many leading retailers reflects the consumer's desire for a running commentary on latest fashion trends and contemporary life styles with which they can identify. Consumers now depend on store activities to provide various forms of consumer education for their personal development in grooming and fashion coordination. They also expect to be stimulated and entertained. When the "show" is less than a hit, consumers can be the kind of critic who is likely to hurt retailers where it hurts most —in the cash register.

*Figure 29. Can you identify the characteristics in this Queen Casuals' ad which satisfy the criteria for an effective advertisement? What level of selling is represented?*

Retail ads should be written in language which reflects a knowledge of the customer. How many retail ads can you find in today's newspaper which reveal that the advertiser really knows who should be the interested reader of his ad?

It is only after accurately selecting the customers for a particular fashion that a retailer can develop a message designed to attain a sales objective. This realization of objectives is the basis for designing an advertising message, and a clear definition of the objective is the only way in which to later evaluate the effectiveness of the communication. In the defining of a promotion objective, the retailer starts by considering the following:

1. What is the present stage of *merchandise-acceptance* by the customer for the product?
2. At what stage is the customer in forming a *decision to buy?*
3. Is the objective of the message one which could possibly have a result *which could be measured?*

Customers are often described as being in a particular stage of acceptance in the making of a decision to buy. The *promotion objective* is affected by an evaluation of which stage describes the maximum number of customers for an offer.

The advertiser will "size-up" his customer to determine what are his strongest motivations to buy. He will try to convince the customer why he should buy this product, why he should buy this brand of product, and why he should buy from this maker. The advertiser should be quite expert on the subject of customer motivations and will develop his copy to reach the motivations of his selected audience.

## MOTIVATIONS

When we first mentioned the needs and wants of customers we referred to them as *motivations.* Motivations to *buy* are reasons why people buy. *Appeals* are reasons to buy given by the *advertiser.* An appeal is based upon a known motivation—and appeals are derived from selling points of products or institutions. We could say that the motivations of customers are the salesperson's target. He uses an appeal as his weapon which is loaded with *selling points* as ammunition.

Motivations are the drives within people which stimulate wants

69

and needs. Customers have individual patterns of motivations and the wise promoter learns what these drives are, and makes a genuine effort to consider the nature of these wants and needs when he designs his messages. The advertiser must be aware of motivations or he cannot develop reasons to buy which will elicit response from customers. *Motivations are the property of people.* They may include convenience, economy, durability, performance, comfort, responsibility status, fear, vanity, self-preservation and, so often in fashion, the desire to appeal to the opposite sex.

The retailer especially must accurately survey his consumer market and his customers in order to identify the nature of demand and merchandise acceptance for different fashion products. He must also be conscious of the *approach* to use with his customers. Figure 30 would have been a daring approach ten years ago. Even when it was published it was one of a series of retail advertising "firsts." The retailer's market can be expressed in terms of its *demographics*—population, education, marital and family status, income —and its *psychographics*—characteristics which describe motiva-

*Figure 30. This lingerie ad has an approach that could almost be called "X-rated"— That is if it had been run ten years ago. It is now considered fun as well as an effective way to advertise this type of fashion product.*

tions to buy. These are investigations which should be undertaken before the decisions on what merchandise to offer, at what price to offer it, and to whom to offer it. It is unfortunate that many retailers who insist they can identify their customers, and then claim that their advertising and promotion is designed to communicate effectively with them, fail at the outset in their attempt to define their market. The defining of the retailer's market is part of his sell ing process which is essential in developing effective appeals and approaches.

An example would be: A retailer who utilizes newspaper ads to present a collection of contemporary women's sportswear by a designer whom the store believes in very strongly. This designer's fashions have appeal for certain customer groups in this store's total group of customers. The messages in these ads should consider the nature and needs of this store's "contemporary woman," how and when she makes her buying decisions, what she reads or listens to, and what her level of acceptances are for certain style trends and fashion "looks."

The advertising message must convince customers who are motivated by a desire to appear different from those who wear volume-produced, popular-priced fashion. The store's assortment of contemporary styles from a leading designer of contemporary fashion has been purchased with this customer in mind.

Many styles have details and features which are exclusive and different. These are selling points which the advertiser can translate into appeals (reasons to buy). Customers who are motivated by the desire to appear different and individual, may respond to this influence of the ad and go to a store which features such exclusive fashions for a closer look.

## SELLING POINTS

The features and characteristics of a product are its selling points. What is good about it? Why would anyone want to buy it? Is it size, color, ease of wearing, design, quality, label, fit, comfort, versatility, shape, fabric, outstanding? The advertiser must study the product with curiosity and knowledge to assemble all the selling points. Then, knowing that he should not overwhelm people into buying, he must select the most outstanding characteristics and present them in their order of importance.

Selling points are the properties of products. The inquiring mind will search for selling points by a thorough study of each product to be advertised. The advertiser, or in this case, the copywriter, will use the brains of everyone around to obtain complete and accurate information. Copywriters also read avidly to keep conversant with every market trend and fashion innovation to become expert on selling points. Their job is to find points of difference that make a client's product unique.

It is hoped that the designers and producers of fashion would build quality selling points into products to afford the consumer greater satisfaction, and to offer the retailer reasons to promote and to advertise merchandise. It is just these qualities which copywriters can then use to develop appeals which will motivate customers to buy.

## APPEALS

When the advertiser has mastered his knowledge of motivations, and becomes thoroughly informed about selling points, he then tries to make a connection between the two factors. When he brings the selling points to the attention of the customer, and those selling points meet the customer's motivations head on, that is the beginning of good advertising. The appeal is the link between the product's selling points and the customer's motivations. The perfect "link-up" is not always likely, but the closer the connection, the better the appeal. It might be well to note again the difference between "customer" and "consumer." A customer is anyone who buys. A consumer is the ultimate user of a product or service.

Effective selling selects appeals from the customer's point of view, or what is most important for his satisfaction.

The seller usually concentrates on a single main appeal. The main appeal is sometimes referred to as the *keynote.* This should be a *unique selling proposition* which stresses the most important reason for the customer to prefer this product at this time. Secondary selling points and appeals may certainly be included, but the keynote should be given priority and emphasis in presentation.

It is the primary appeal that can be relied upon to do the big job of interesting and influencing the customer.

The main appeal is the bridge between product and customer. It is used to stimulate *attention, interest, desire* and hopefully, *action.*

## APPROACH

The experienced advertiser or salesperson knows that the way he presents his sales message is an important factor in potential customer response. The manner of presentation is called *approach.* In personal selling, the master salesperson shapes and changes appeal and approach in response to feedback from the customer. In advertising, the selected appeal and approach has to be carefully developed from accurate customer profiles of the group of customers to which an advertisement is directed.

*The approach is the way in which the appeal is presented,* and the selection of approach is the decision of the advertiser.

An example is the television commercial. Because people look upon television as a source of entertainment, advertising in this medium is often presented with an amusing and entertaining appoach.

Advertising approaches fall into three categories.

1. Factual (direct selling information)
2. Narrative (story development which includes transition to the product)
3. Projective (puts the customer into a situation which features use and benefits of product)

An approach can be developed in one of three ways:

1. Rational
2. Emotional
3. Combination of rational and emotional

Figures 31 and 32 present two main approaches in a fashion ad.

Many fashion advertisements fall into the third or combination category. However, it would be an unusual approach which would be precisely half emotional and half rational. Usually, in the combined approach there is emphasis on either emotional or rational treatment. The exception to the rule will be found in trade advertising in which it is not uncommon for the approach to be entirely rational. When appeals are based on practical motivations such as economy, profit or durability, a completely factual approach is appropriate.

It is the consideration and application of all of the aforementioned —motivations to buy, appeals, selling points, approach—which constitute the *selling process* (Figure 33).

*Figures 31 and 32. Which ad uses the factual approach? Which one is imaginative in approach?*

ralph lauren...a chap who means business

His softened navy wool pinstripe. With a vest, classic styling... all the perfectionist details Ralph's based his own career on. The kind of monopoly on style that's earned him the coveted Coty Hall of Fame Award... incorporated into one self-assured new candidate for The Peterborough® Man. Crisps by Ralph Lauren. Peruse the letter of reference in the breast pocket, you'll discover a man with a point of view. But then, you are too. 275.00. The Men's Store, Escalator Level, New York.

# bloomingdale's
## the men's store

1000 Third Avenue, New York. 355-5900. Open late Monday and Thursday evenings.
Also available in Fresh Meadows, Stamford, Bergen County, Short Hills, Garden City, Jenkintown, White Plains and Tysons Corner.

*Figure 31.*

# Which of these suits do you prefer?

## *Be careful; it's a loaded question.*

Let's run down a list of possible wrong answers.

**1.** The one on the right. I like a sporty look. That double-d-ring **throat** belt is a bit of all right, old chap.

**2.** The one on the left. It's dressy enough for the office, but still casual. Bellows pockets are news, right?

**3.** I'll take them both. One for week-ends, one for the work-week.

We gave you a **clue** in answer #2. "Bellows pockets." Now study our sketches once more, Sherlock. Ah, you got it! These are not two different suits. This is **one** (very different) suit. With a label you're hearing about more and more: **Country Britches**.

Pure wool, of course, in an earthy-brown minicheck called "end on end tickweave" by our buyer, who speaks **menswear-ese** as fluently as English.

You can see on this page how versatile it is. You can't see the straight leg trousers, the buttoned back vent, the change pocket with buttoned flap. And you can't see how fine this new two-in-one suit will look on you. Come **prove it** to yourself in Altman's Men's Store, main floor. Sizes 37 to 44 reg. 38 to 42 short. 39 to 44 long. 175.00.

A **smart** man like you is just the customer we want.

B Altman & Co

Altman's Men's Store, main floor.
Fifth Avenue, White Plains, Manhasset, N.Y.,
Short Hills, Ridgewood/Paramus, N.J., St. Davids, Pa.

*Figure 32.*

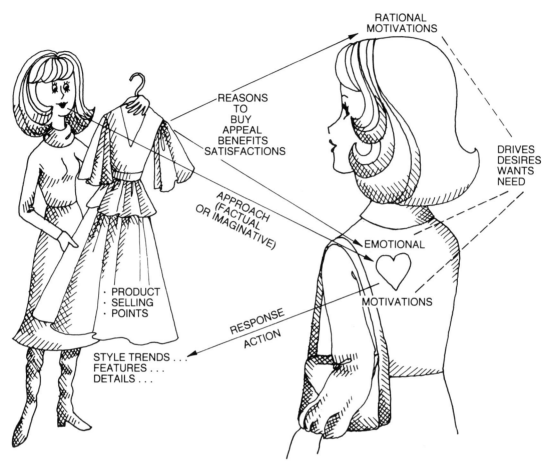

*Figure 33. The selling process is dependent upon a thorough understanding of what customers want and what satisfactions products have to offer. The "connector" is the appeal or "reason to buy" backed by convincing selling points, which are presented in an approach suitable to the nature of the product and the type of customer in your market.*

## MERCHANDISE-ACCEPTANCE CURVE

Every type of merchandise—every individual product—is likely to move through various stages of public acceptance during its "life." When it is first introduced and its acceptance is generally of a limited nature, it is said to be in a stage of *pioneering*. If and when it wins more universal acceptance, it proceeds to a stage of *acceptance*. Thereafter, unless changes or improvements are made in the product, it is likely to pass to a stage of *decline* and eventually, perhaps, even into a stage of *abandonment.* This movement of a product through the four stages of pioneering, acceptance, decline and abandonment could be represented graphically by a *merchandise-acceptance curve.*\*

All products do not travel the stages at the same speed. Each item may remain for varying lengths of time in any of the four stages, depending upon the nature of the article and the rate at which it gains or loses customer acceptance. Some products, such as novelty apparel and various fashion fads may complete their life cycle in a few weeks or, at most, in a few months. Others such as major apparel items that embody design features, may move more slowly through each of the stages over a period of several years. Therefore, the merchandise-acceptance curves of different products are likely to take a slightly different form or shape. All of the curves, however, include four stages.

The merchandise-acceptance curve attempts to visualize the position that an item of merchandise holds in public favor at any given time. It is *not measurement* of acceptance, but rather *a method of visualizing the comparative levels of acceptance.* Accordingly, the merchandise-acceptance curve can help determine the type of advertising that the product warrants or requires at that particular time. An awareness of which merchandise is being introduced, is flourishing, is waning, or is dying, suggests whether the store should employ prestige, regular-price-line, special-price, or clearance advertising. (See Figure 34.) It also suggests the selection of appeals and approach. It therefore keeps a store from using a type of advertising—or any advertising—too early or too late.

For example, the visualization of the merchandise-acceptance of a particular product may prevent an advertiser from advertising this item after it has passed out of favor. Such an effort would be futile and wasteful because no amount of advertising can sell merchandise that customers have indicated they do not want. A product that has lost its appeal to customers can be revived only if it is changed or improved so substantially that it wins new acceptance and thereby literally begins a new "life," or new cycle. The "cycle" could also be viewed in the following manner.

---

\*Charles M. Edwards, Jr., Russel A. Brown, *Retail Advertising and Sales Promotion* (New Jersey, 1964), p. 166.

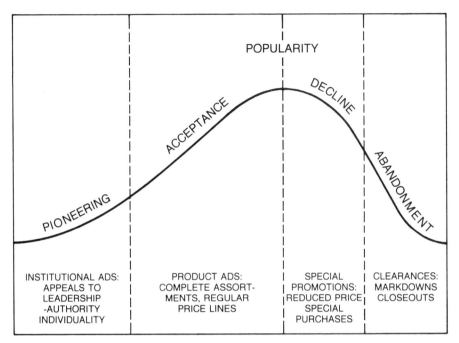

POPULARITY

DECLINE

ACCEPTANCE

ABANDONMENT

PIONEERING

| INSTITUTIONAL ADS: APPEALS TO LEADERSHIP -AUTHORITY INDIVIDUALITY | PRODUCT ADS: COMPLETE ASSORT-MENTS, REGULAR PRICE LINES | SPECIAL PROMOTIONS: REDUCED PRICE SPECIAL PURCHASES | CLEARANCES: MARKDOWNS CLOSEOUTS |

*Figure 34. Merchandise-acceptance curve and appropriate advertising used for each phase.*

## PIONEERING STAGE

Customers are not aware of the designer, the styles or a desire for such merchandise. In this case the promotion objective might be to introduce and activate interest.

## ACCEPTANCE STAGE

Customers are in the process of being exposed to several merchandise offerings of a similar nature. They are becoming aware of appeals and features of the products and interest and desire are being increased. The promotion objective here could be to heighten desire and work on motivations to buy.

## POPULARITY STAGE

Customers have begun to make decisions to buy and are in the process of shopping for the "right merchandise at the right price." The promotion objective should be to persuade customers that your version of merchandise, and that your store is their right decision —and why it is.

**DECLINE**

Customers have been buying the merchandise and a market has been created. But there are signs of a leveling off and decline in demand. The promotion objective in this stage is to reinforce their choice of merchandise and store, and to build and retain customer loyalty offering promotions at reduced prices from special purchases.

**ABANDONMENT**

Time to consider close-out and clearance sales. The advertising should only feature previously *wanted* items at a substantial markdown.

## THE STAGE HELPS DETERMINE THE COPY KEYNOTE

When a product is first introduced, it is presented to customers through advertising that accents the newness of the merchandise and the alertness of the store.

As the item gains increasing acceptance, it is generally offered through regular-price-line advertisements that emphasize the selling points of the merchandise, as well as through prestige advertisements that call attention to the complete assortments carried by the store.

When the merchandise wins such universal approval that is sought by everybody, including people in medium- and low-income groups, and is offered on a *price* basis in a multitude of stores, it is announced widely through special-promotion advertising which stresses price concessions on merchandise from stock as well as upon special purchases of manufacturers' surpluses. At this point, the product is likely to decline steadily in favor unless it is modified or improved in such a way that it reverts to the pioneering stage.

## APPEAL AND APPROACH AT
## VARIOUS MARKET LEVELS

It is not reasonable to generalize about appeal and approach in terms of *market level.* It *is* reasonable to assume that the "professional buyer" for a producer is more interested in facts than in the projections of the seller. Rational reasons to buy, presented with a factual approach, are necessary when a buyer is contemplating the purchase of $75,000 worth of fabric for garment production. The ultimate consumer *buying for herself* may like to hear what could happen when she wears *this* dress, or uses *this* perfume. "Your boss will love you if you design your new collection with Royal Fabrics," has not been an effective appeal in *trade* advertising and selling.

We might now realize that a clearly identified promotion objective for an advertisement, (or any promotion activity, program or campaign) is only as effective as the retailer's ability to understand the present stage of wants and needs of his customers. He must know "where his customers are"—in respect to their present stage of acceptance and decision to buy. There are some cases where those retailers who are usually not innovators in introducing fashion trends, know that very few of their customers are ever interested in most products which are in the pioneering stage. An examination of merchandise-acceptance of certain other products, however, could reveal that many of their customers are interested in the pioneering stage of just these products. The retailer must consider *what* he is selling and to whom, when he defines promotional objectives.

# 6

# Media Planning
# for Fashion Advertising

An advertisement or a commercial relies on a *medium* or a combi-
of media to transmit messages to potential customers. *Media planning* is a process of selecting media time and space to aid in the
attainment of marketing, merchandising, and sales objectives. The
advertiser has a choice of various types of mass media each of
which have characteristics and assets of their own in reaching readers, listeners or viewers. An advertiser *buys space* in *print* media or
*buys time* in *broadcast* media. He pays a specific rate for this service based upon the frequency, total amount, and special requests of
his purchases. The mass media designed for public information are:

1. *Newspapers, Magazines, Outdoor Advertising (Billboards)*
   and *Transit Advertising* which sell *space* to advertisers for
   their advertisements.
2. *Radio* and *Television* broadcasters will sell *time* on their
   programs to advertisers for their commercials.
3. Advertisers can create their own medium through the use of
   *direct mail* and the advertiser produces various types of direct mail advertising which is delivered by the U.S. Postal
   Service for the price of the postage. Direct mail is not considered mass media for public information. It is a direct medium
   produced by the advertiser himself.

*Figure 35.*

Except for the large primary producers of fashion (Monsanto, Du Pont, Burlington Mills) and a smaller number of secondary producers (Playtex, Cluett-Peabody, Hanes) and several of the retail giants (Sears, J.C. Penney, Montgomery-Ward), relatively few fash-. ion firms can afford to use media in the quantity and quality they might wish, to communicate with customers. Marshall McLuhan's* attempt to create a basic law of the nature of media simplified media analysis and selection to "the medium is the message." There is no argument if we interpret McLuhan's idea to mean that the impact of appeals and approaches in advertising messages can be affected by the selection of media (and the medium's audience).

This chapter shall discuss the basic analyses and criteria which fashion firms on all three levels, primary, secondary and retail, use to select their media mix. The use of a combination of media (media mix or multimedia) recognizes that even if the same messages

*Marshall McLuhan, *Understanding Media: The Extension of Man* (New York, 1964).

reach customers in more than one medium—the qualities of the medium and its individual characteristics of how, when, and where messages are transmitted and received affect the nature of the message.

The fashion advertiser must decide which of these media will best suit his purposes. A raw materials manufacturer may find that he can send *his* sales message most effectively by direct mail. He may also use trade newspapers and/or magazines to reach his audience. Raw materials producers are interested in selling their products to apparel manufacturers. They will select trade media which can reach them. A raw materials producer may also be interested in influencing consumers to buy finished garments which are made from his products. In this case he will select *consumer* media which will reach the ultimate consumer. The marketer of primary fashion products and the merchandiser of fashion apparel and accessories must develop media strategies and tactics in his promotional planning. The media plan is an essential part of the success of advertising and promotion. Product characteristics, channels of distribution, and pricing are also basic considerations.

The informed advertiser does not select a medium merely because his competitors are using it—or because it is an accepted method for his market level. He does not try to outdo the competition in the medium they use; rather, he investigates all available media to see which best reach his audience and which *he can use most* effectively.

Relatively few retailers of fashion have promotional appropriations which can budget large amounts of money for all media. The retailer must develop an individual formula for media planning and selection based upon his own research and experience. Most retailers have found newspapers to be their most effective choice in terms of consumer response and cost. The trend, however, is to plan more of a media mix and many retailers large and small have been very successful with radio, direct mail and *local* television.

For any advertiser on any market level the criteria for selection of media would involve a study of individual media assets which consider:

- The composition and quantity of the audience *coverage*
- *Response* or *rate-of-return* effect indicated by the experience of the advertiser or substantive data supplied by the medium

- Product or institution *name penetration* or recall effect produced by frequency and repetition of message in the particular medium

The consideration of the media assets above would have to include a qualitative and quantitative analysis of the medium's cost-per-thousand contacts. We will deal with this as a major consideration later in this chapter.

If we acknowledge that *coverage, response,* and *penetration* are primary considerations for media selection, we should expand our conceptual analysis further.

Most advertisers are interested in selecting media which will communicate or "cover" all of those who constitute their active and high-potential customers. Coverage refers to the ability of a medium to contact a certain audience group through its circulation or broadcast signal. There is no way of knowing who is actually reading, listening, or viewing print or broadcast media at any given time. A medium's *reach* is a description of the unduplicated number of people in the medium's coverage exposed to a message at least once in a period of time (usually four weeks). Reach is therefore always smaller than coverage.

The actual reach of a medium is a result of its cumulative effect over a period of time. Therefore its *cumulative reach* or "cume" is more than its *one-time reach.* The cume, however, is also smaller than the total coverage.

If a retailer is running radio spots on a daytime talk show, how many *additional* or *unduplicated* homes will it reach by buying time on an evening news program? The reach may not increase by using more radio commercials in this case—but the *frequency of exposure* to the retailer's sales messages may be increased to affect the response. Frequency is defined as the number of times an individual or household is exposed to a medium within a given time period.

The *effective* audience or effective circulation must be considered in reach. What percentage of the coverage would your message appeal to? How many of the individuals reached by the message are likely prospects as customers for this offer? In this store? The large department store with its wider and deeper classifications of merchandise, and variety of styles and assortments, could reasonably estimate a greater *effective* reach from a medium with general coverage (rather than one with very selective audiences) than could a highly specialized boutique with a specific target market.

In addition to reach and frequency, the media planner must consider *continuity,* which refers to how advertising is scheduled over a designated period of time. The timing of ads or commercials "continuously" or separated in time is involved.

A media planner certainly could not hope to be able to finance media objectives which called for *maximum* reach and *frequency within a specified time.* Rating points describe reach in terms of the percentage of TV households a television station reaches with a program compared with a total of all TV households in a market area. Media strategy most often is a balance of the amounts of rating-point reach and frequency called *gross rating points,* arrived at by multiplying the total number of rating points a program bearing a commercial has from each station in an area-times-frequency (GRP = RP $\times$ F) for a given period of time. The advertiser's success in media planning will depend upon his ability to describe his target market in terms of the demographic characteristics and psychographic attributes of big target customers. He will have to consider levels and stages of merchandise-acceptance and product-usage. The advertiser's marketing goals and sales objectives are vital factors in media strategy and planning. The factors of frequency, reach and continuity will determine the *success* as well as the *cost* of attaining objectives—consequently, the design of an effective media plan is vital in any marketing and/or merchandising program.

## CHECKLIST FOR MEDIA SELECTION

The following is a checklist which summarizes criteria for the selection of media—and adds a few more important considerations.

1. *The type of customer* sought by the advertiser—Is this message for a prospect, regular customer or inactive customer?
2. *The type of business* the advertiser is conducting—Is the emphasis on quality, price, service?
3. *The characteristics of the product involved*—Does it have general or limited appeal? Is it a new product; an established product with a new feature; highly competitive or exclusive; a classic?
4. *The nature of the message*—Are we interested in selling pro-

ducts, creating advance interest in them, disseminating useful information; selling the institution, personnel or services behind the product?

5. *The appropriateness of the medium* for the product and producer—The level of acceptance of the medium and frame of mind of its audience when exposed to it. Would an advertisement for sexy lingerie in the *Reader's Digest* do as well as it would in *Cosmopolitan* Magazine?

6. *Location of the business*—Is the location in a high or low traffic area; easily accessible or not?

7. *Location of audience*—Where does the advertiser's business come from? The whereabouts of the customer in relation to *circulation of the medium.*

8. *The cost of available media*—The actual and relative cost of advertising in different media must be considered. The media buyer is mainly concerned with the *cost-per-thousand contacts, CPM,* (readers, listeners, viewers). The cost-per-thousand contacts are determined by dividing the medium's audience (the number of thousands) into the cost for space or time. The media buyer must also consider what part of the total audience is really his potential customers, from whom he can expect the maximum *rate of response.* This is called the *effective* audience or circulation and *true* or actual *CPM* is calculated by using this figure. Direct mail is one medium where the advertiser selects the audience. (Usually, the more selective a medium is, the higher its cost.)

Example of how to calculate CPM: If a magazine has a circulation of 1,000,000 and its one-page rate is $10,000, the CPM is calculated in this way:

$$\frac{\text{Cost of Space in \$}}{\text{Circulation in } thousands} = \frac{\$10,000}{1,000} = \$10 \text{ CPM}$$

In addition to a preliminary application of the criteria above, the advertiser should determine which media are *most* productive from an analysis of his own past sales experience, or by questioning buyers, salespeople and customers themselves through interview or questionnaires. There are many methods of more formal research which help the advertiser to determine which media customers rely

*Figure 36. An example of how a major fashion magazine promotes its media assets to potential advertisers. (Courtesy of SEVENTEEN Magazine.)*

on, and when and how they use each medium in the group they prefer.

Gross rating points (GRP) is an analytical tool, which indicates the number of listeners or viewers in a radio or television audience during a specific time period as a percentage of all of the potential audience in the market. GRP refers to total or gross number of rating points delivered by the advertiser's radio or television schedule. To review—GRP is equal to: Total rating points multiplied by frequency ($GRP = RP \times F$) in a designated time period.

The media themselves spend much effort and money in *media research* which is available to advertisers. Naturally you would expect each medium to present data which would encourage the advertiser to choose *it*. (Figure 36). Nevertheless, a comparative survey of available media research can be useful as a guide to the advertiser. There is also much existing information published by the United States Government, Chambers of Commerce, trade associations and other business agencies which can be studied in the selection of media. More on this in our section on the cost of media (page 89).

## RELATIVE IMPORTANCE OF MEDIA FOR DIFFERENT LEVELS OF THE FASHION INDUSTRY

It is useful to arrive at some general concept on the relative importance of media for the different types of firms in the fashion business. Of course there are many exceptions because there are so many different types of firms in each level. For example, the broad category of retailers would include: large multi-unit chains, metropolitan area department stores, department store branches, small city and town department stores, specialty chains, specialty shops, boutiques. In addition each of these types of stores might have different objectives. Some would emphasize quality, low prices, exclusiveness, discount prices, fashion leadership, or fashion "following."

Despite these variations most retailers find local newspapers a productive advertising medium; others use direct mail or radio or a combination of these. Figure 37 is an attempt to generalize on the relative importance of media for different firms on each market level of the fashion industry.

| | BRAND-NAME* | UN-BRANDED |
|---|---|---|
| RAW MATERIALS PRODUCERS | 1. DIRECT MAIL<br>2. TRADE NEWSPAPERS AND MAGAZINES<br>3. CONSUMER MAGAZINES AND NEWSPAPERS<br>4. TV AND RADIO | 1. DIRECT MAIL<br>2. TRADE NEWSPAPERS AND MAGAZINES |
| APPAREL MANU-FACTURERS | 1. DIRECT MAIL<br>2. TRADE NEWSPAPERS AND MAGAZINES<br>3. CONSUMER NEWSPAPERS AND MAGAZINES<br>4. TV AND RADIO | 1. DIRECT MAIL<br>2. TRADE NEWSPAPERS AND MAGAZINES |
| | LARGE STORES | SMALL STORES |
| RETAILERS | 1. CONSUMER NEWSPAPERS<br>2. DIRECT MAIL<br>3. TV AND RADIO | 1. CONSUMER NEWSPAPERS<br>2. DIRECT MAIL |

*Larger producers who spend money to advertise their identity for *brand-recognition, acceptance and preference.*

*Figure 37.*

## THE COST OF ADVERTISING MEDIA

Who is interested in advertising media—its cost, its basis for rates? At every level of the fashion industry, each key executive needs some knowledge of the structure of media costs for he or she may certainly be involved in media selection and buying decisions and in the evaluation of media. As an example, a department store buyer will be required to know how and where her advertising budget is to be used. The recommendation of this decision is frequently part of her "request for advertising."

When an executive understands a function of his work, he tends to make sound objective decisions. Therefore it is not the exclusive privilege of an advertising manager to be knowledgeable about media. Newspapers and magazines, outdoor advertising and transit advertising have different bases upon which they establish advertising costs to the advertiser.

## NEWSPAPERS

Since newspapers are read in 87 percent of United States households and by 81 percent of all persons over 18*, this becomes a most vital channel of communication. There are but very few remote cross-roads in this country not served by a local newspaper—morning, evening, Sunday, weekly, special interest, or by some combination of these. There are over 9000 of these in the United States.

*Newspaper Advertising Bureau (NAB)

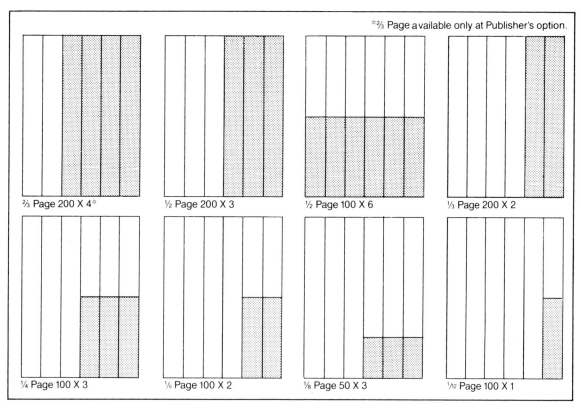

*⅔ Page available only at Publisher's option.

⅔ Page 200 X 4*

½ Page 200 X 3

½ Page 100 X 6

⅓ Page 200 X 2

¼ Page 100 X 3

⅙ Page 100 X 2

⅛ Page 50 X 3

1/12 Page 100 X 1

*Figure 38. New page formats for two of the nation's most prominent newspapers. Left:* THE NEW YORK TIMES *(standard size) is 6 columns for news, 9 for advertising. Right: The* DAILY NEWS *(tabloid size) is now 5 columns for news, 6 for advertising.*

The large or standard newspaper such as *The New York Times* or *Chicago Tribune,* and the tabloid such as the New York *Daily News* or *Women's Wear Daily (WWD),* vary in size. The standard size page usually has a depth of between 280 to 300 lines to the column. Each paper specifies its exact size in its rate schedule which is available to all advertisers. A full page in the standard size paper usually runs to 300 lines per column. The column in a standard or tabloid page is from 1¾ to 2¼ inches wide.

The tabloid size page is usually 5 or 6 columns wide and the columns run about 1200 lines deep. Thus, a full page is 1000 to 1200 lines. A "line" in a newspaper is an *agate* line, usually just called *lines* or *lineage*. There are fourteen lines to the inch. Therefore an agate line is newspaper space 1/14 of an inch, one column wide. An ad 150 lines deep, 3 columns wide is a 450 line ad, or 150 on 3 (150 lines on 3 columns).

Newspapers have changed the number of *columns* of news and of advertising in many instances. As previously discussed, there are two sizes of newspapers generally with very few exceptions: the *large* or *standard* page, and the *tabloid* size page. In both sizes of newspapers there have been changes in columns.

In September of 1976, two of the nation's better known papers, *The New York Times,* a standard sized paper, and the *Daily News,* a tabloid, changed their column widths. *The Times* changed from eight news columns to six. However, its advertising space is sold at nine columns to the page. Page overall dimensions did not change, but the total number of lines has increased from 2400 (8 columns × 300 lines) to 2700 (9 columns × 300 lines).

The *Daily News* changed from six news columns to five; but advertising space runs six columns wide. Therefore, its full-page size is now 1200 lines, or 6 columns × 200 lines. The page layouts reproduced here illustrate the new standard and tabloid page sizes (see Figure 38). Such changes are not limited to the papers we mention. A number of other papers in Chicago, Washington, Cleveland, Pittsburgh and Denver have adopted the "six-on-nine" column plan as now used by *The New York Times.* Such uniformity facilitates preparation of *national* campaign advertising placement by manufacturers and producers. Newspapers are still the principal medium for *retail* advertising, though not the only medium. Radio and television are used by many retailers, but not to the extent of the use of newspapers.

It is well to consider the reason for the heavy use of newspapers for retail advertising. People read their newspapers for *News.* That includes news of where to shop. Such news has an element of immediacy—*Now* is the time to buy!

A fact worth noting is that several standard size newspapers sell space in their classified section on the basis of ten columns to the page. A look at *The New York Times* will illustrate their use of six columns for news; nine columns for advertising; and ten columns for classified ads. It sounds much more complicated than it is, but it is wise to know these factors. The media buyer often uses a standard method of evaluating various newspaper costs. It is called *milline.* The *milline rate* is a unit for measuring the rate of newspaper advertising space compared to circulation; the cost of having each *agate line* presented to 1,000,000 readers. It is derived in the following way:

$$\text{Milline} = \frac{1,000,000 \times \text{Line Rate}}{\text{Amount of Circulation}}$$

Knowledge of space in newspapers is important not only to the media buyer, but also to the merchandise manager and buyer who should know something about the amount of space his ad will occupy before it is seen in the publication. A simple query and brief lesson in the advertising department should show a buyer what kind of space a three-hundred line or twelve-hundred line ad will occupy, and how much of the budget is going to be spent on each advertisement.

Changes in newspaper column layouts should be observed carefully. It is the present time that such changes are taking place.

Another factor one should have in mind is the immediate understanding when an advertising manager speaks to you and says, for example, "You have 900 lines in next Thursday's *New York Times,*" you would think of this as a third of a page. Contrary to this, if the ad manager speaks of a third of a page in the same paper, you know that the bill for space will be for 900 lines. Thus it becomes important to develop a familiarity with language, page sizes and rates. The page layouts in Figure 38 are worth studying for this purpose. Because rates are constantly changing, it would not be practical to specify them here.

The basic cost in a newspaper rate schedule entitles the advertiser to a run-of-paper position, usually referred to as the R.O.P. rate. This puts the advertisement in any place in the paper, chosen by the publisher. When an advertiser specifies the position or page he wants for his ad, he pays a *preferred position,* or higher rate. Of course, such preference can be exercised only upon availability. Many long-term contracts for such positions give priority to the contracting advertisers and are renewable upon expiration. Choice positions can include specific up-front pages or possibly back page.

An advertiser may *request* a "good position, above fold" or "if possible, outside columns" without the extra charge, but this assures the advertiser of no consistency of position.

## MAGAZINES

Magazines sell space by the page or fraction of page. A page, half-page, quarter-page, etc., can be bought by the advertiser. Space in the magazine is sold often by the column or part of the column also. The measurement of advertising space by lines is not used in magazines. Magazine rates are determined by *circulation* which is audited by the Audit Bureau of Circulations (ABC) a recognized certification service.

In magazines, an advertiser can reach a nationally distributed market or he may choose specific areas through sectional editions offered by many magazines. One magazine appropriately once named this option, "magazones." These zones vary in geographical size and each magazine gives the advertiser precise information as to geographical and circulation coverage, by zone. Thus, a comparatively smaller advertiser may find value with sufficient budget to include magazines in his media plan.

## DIRECT MAIL

This is a fast growing medium for all market levels of the fashion industry. In as much as direct-mail advertising is planned, produced, and financed by the advertiser there are no standard rates available. The CPM of direct mail is very high and must include creative, production, and handling costs as well as postage. The *rate-of-response* and *rate-of-return,* when the mailing list is *effective* is also very high, and carries with its sales message the possibility of *mail orders* from customers. It is easy to see why it is possible to have the most effective reach in all media from direct mail. In this medium, coverage is determined by the advertisers own mailing list, and the proportion of reach to coverage is very high. Because of this it is an ideal medium for *trade,* or *retail levels of selling,* and it is utilized by fashion producers and manufacturers for trade advertising, and by retailers of all types and sizes in their catalogs, brochures, flyers, statement enclosures and public relations announcements. On the *national* level it is used for test marketing new products, more so for packaged merchandise than fashion. An example is the free sample of a new bar of soap you might receive in your "occupant" mail.

## OUTDOOR AND TRANSIT ADVERTISING

Advertising space is sold for billboards and above-the-seats space in subways, trains and buses. Rates are determined by the estimated number of impressions on people who move through the specific locations and size of space. Major retailers, producers and manufacturers use outdoor and transit advertising in a limited way for special offers and seasonal promotions.

## TELEVISION

Television advertising has proved to be most influential of all media in many respects. Its influence is incredible. According to the Television Bureau of Advertising, more than 95 percent of all American households, or over sixty million, have at least one television set and close to 60 percent of these are color sets. Through network broadcasting, with over 500 stations in all but the small cities and towns, millions of homes can be reached with measurable impact very quickly. With a one-minute commercial, in a single program, on a single network (CBS, NBC, ABC) it is possible to reach more than eleven million homes. The average viewing time in each of these households is over six hours a day. This is coverage which would be of interest to the producers and manufacturers of fashion but not necessary for retailers who need local coverage in their own trading area.

The cost of these programs, however, on a network basis is excessive for the budgets and purposes of most primary producers and apparel manufacturers. Except for the giants of the industry, there is relatively little network television advertising by the fashion industry. It is said that the minimum cost for a half-hour evening network show for just time and talent may run over $250,000. The cost of a single commercial on network television in *prime* time can be as much as $60,000, and $100,000 for a full minute. On top of that cost are writers, production costs and promotion expenses which can be as much as $35,000. It is not economical advertising for most. It *is* expensive, but productive (with very low CPM) for the advertiser whose product and objectives are suited to *mass* audience coverage.

As an example, a one-minute or sixty-second single spot commercial on network television telecast in the course of the professional sports spectacular, such as the World Series of Baseball, has been sold for $250,000, and costs keep going up each year.

Television advertising falls into two main categories:

1. *Network or Sponsorship Advertising*—Sponsored commercials are part of a scheduled program and are run at the beginning, middle and end. In some programs there are participating or shared sponsorship among several advertisers.

2. *Spot Advertising*—A spot is a broadcast commercial (radio as well as television) which is from ten to sixty seconds not related to an accompanying program. This can be national or local. With spot commercials the advertiser may use selective or target markets. Spots are sold in segments of ten, twenty, thirty seconds, or one minute.

All rates for television advertising are based on time of broadcast. The "heart" of viewing attention varies from station to station, but generally *prime time* is from 7 P.M. to 11 P.M. The hour before and after this choice period is referred to as *fringe time.* There are other classifications possible and some stations break the time segments into as many as five.

The technique and details of the creation of good television advertising should never be in the hands of any but top professionals. At such costs as those previously mentioned, an error in judgment is less than tolerable and every precaution to be efficient and effective should be taken.

## RADIO

Especially for the retailer of fashion, radio is an excellent value for his media dollar. It has an ability over a segment of time to reach a substantial audience, with great selectivity as to time, type of programming, and frequency. The type of audience can be selected for very high-quality coverage, from teenagers at play or "study" to their fathers commuting to and from work in their automobiles.

Local radio advertising, according to the Federal Communications Commission, constitutes about 64 percent of radio time sales while spot sales are about 30 percent. This leaves about 6 percent for network radio sales. Time for advertisers is sold on radio in ten-, twenty-, thirty-second or one-minute spots. Segments of programs are also sold by many stations—mostly the FM group. Premium time is often called *drive* or *traffic* time, news time, or weather reports.

## MEDIA RESEARCH SERVICES

One thing above all is certain. To evaluate the costs involved in the use of any medium, newspapers, magazine, direct mail, outdoor transit, television or radio requires no guesswork whatsoever. It can be done objectively and statistically by obtaining the facts of the market coverage from media studies and reports which are available to the advertiser from media research services. The most prominent of these are: *A.C. Nielsen Co.,* who provides audience measurement for individual local television markets (NSI) and national audience measurements for all network programs (NTI); *Home Testing Institute,* who measures audiences which prefer certain programs; *Target Group Index (TGI)* and *W. R. Simmons,* who provide syndicated reports of demographic characteristics of market groups in terms of product and brand usage; the *Standard Rate and Data Service Directories (SRDS)* list media in all print and broadcast categories by geographical and descriptive classification; *Trendex Reports,* who describes and evaluates audience characteristics for independent consumer research.

There are other services which evaluate copy, readership, recall and impact of mass media. *Daniel Starch and Staff,* issues syndicated reports that measure levels of print advertising readership, viewer impression studies and immediate recall plus other types of copy research and testing; *Burke,* prepares special studies on day-after recall; *Arbitron (ARB),* is a radio and television testing service which measures audiences in selected markets; *Gallup and Robinson (TPI),* measures attention-getting ability of commercials and reception of selling points.

The resourceful advertiser has other sources of current, established material: Directories, newspaper and trade journal listings and announcements, trade association reference material and government statistical information are just a few.

Part of any comprehensive advertising budget might also include independent studies which are possible and recommended. These will either confirm or correct information supplied by the medium, and be a valuable part of media-plan decisions designed to match media to markets.

# THE CHARACTERISTICS OF MAJOR FASHION ADVERTISING MEDIA

## NEWSPAPERS

There is much to say about the assets of newspapers as an advertising medium. Retailers on a local level are by far the greatest users of newspaper advertising in the fashion industry. Primary fashion producers and secondary apparel manufacturers are often involved in this medium through cooperative advertising which will be discussed in a later chapter. The retail store regards the newspaper as a local medium with the ability to reach his target customer on a local level. The newspaper ad can be a product of the retailer's own design and personality. It is usually less costly to produce newspaper ads, than to produce radio or television commercials, magazine ads or direct mail.

Retailers have been spending from 50 to 75 percent of their total advertising allocation in newspapers. The consumer still relies on newspaper advertising for most of his information on fashion trends and product knowledge. The retail newspaper advertisement has had a long record of success in generating store traffic and profitable sales. The variety and numbers of newspapers provide in combination and by selection of special zone (split-run) editions an opportunity for effective reach. There is no limit to the amount of good space available for advertisers—for newspapers will print more pages in peak periods. The flexibility of size and design are custom features which any advertiser who is creative can have. Despite increasing costs of space and production, CPM is relatively low and color is now available in almost all of the major daily newspapers.

Newspapers are considered by most readers as musts in the home and have the advantage of being read by each member of a household once and possibly "picked up again."

The difficulties in using newspapers include some waste circulation, for despite the variety and zoned circulation runs, the audience cannot be "targeted" as in direct mail, for example. The small budget advertiser faces enormous competition from larger and more creatively conceived advertisements. The nature of newsprint and the rapid printing techniques utilized are often not capable of producing a good quality of reproduction for fashion illustration and photography. This is a problem for small retailers who cannot hope for much assistance in advertising design from the smaller newspaper.

Nevertheless, newspapers if used effectively are a flexible medium which can produce great results for retailers in customer interest, store traffic and over-the-counter sales. The advertiser knows the nature of his audience and the quantity of coverage (which is certified by the Audit Bureau of Circulations, ABC). It is the advertiser's job to determine his own best use of size, timing, frequency, format/style, and merchandise offered to realize his sales and institutional objectives from newspaper advertising. The producers and manufacturers of fashion use *trade* newspapers for their trade advertising programs. There are trade papers (and magazines) for virtually every market and merchandise classification of raw materials and fashion products.

## MAGAZINES

Magazines are read leisurely and do not carry the urgency in their advertising expected of and found in newspapers. They may be read again and again, and are kept by some long after the issue date. Because of the better quality of the paper used by magazines as compared to newspaper stock, the printing process can be finer. A considerable amount of fashion advertising in magazines is done in color. Color has been found to get more reader attention than does black and white.

Magazines as a medium for advertising may be useful for *national* advertisers of fashion, such as a producer of textiles, Dan River Mills; or an apparel manufacturer, Jonathan Logan. National advertisers of fashion are a relatively limited group, however, and the trend in national advertising of fashion goes beyond the advertising of products and more toward featuring institutional, brand name or "family-of-products" themes. *Retail* advertising in magazines would generally be limited to only the leading retail chains with branches throughout the nation (Sears, J.C. Penney, Montgomery-Ward) and those major retailers with recognition and reputations which go beyond their own local trading areas (Bergdorf-Goodman, I. Magnin, Saks Fifth Avenue, Neiman-Marcus). For prestige and image objectives these retailers find it effective to do *retail* advertising in a *national* medium such as magazines.

The advertising by producers and fashion manufacturers in magazines is more likely to consist of imaginative and projective appeals with an emotional approach. They are largely institutional in objective. This in contrast to newspaper advertising by retailers for more immediate product objectives. Even retailer's ads in magazines are more institutional and contain more imaginative appeals and approaches than do their newspaper ads.

For the national advertiser, magazines rank as a second medium to television. But for fashion producers of raw materials and apparel manufacturers, the fashion magazine *(Seventeen, Glamour, Mademoiselle, Bazaar, Vogue, Gentlemen's Quarterly)* or the general and special interest consumer magazine which features fashion *(Cosmopolitan, Esquire, The New York Times Magazine Section)* is the most favored advertising medium.

## DIRECT MAIL

*Direct-mail advertising* is a medium of advertising that is sent through the mail. It is a most important member of the advertising media family. If a leaflet is placed on a store countertop, that is *direct advertising.* But if the leaflet is sent by mail that is *direct-mail advertising.* Physically the two items may be the same. However, the difference is in the way they are distributed.

Generally, the first form of advertising most firms use when they start into business are letters, flyers and other forms of direct-mail advertising. No matter how large they become or how many other types of advertising they use, direct mail is usually one of them. It is for most firms in the fashion industry perhaps 5 to 10 percent of the total budget for advertising. For some retailers it will constitute as much as 75 percent. The trend to catalog and mail-order selling through direct-mail advertising by department stores is growing.

*Direct mail* should not be confused with *mail-order.* Direct mail is an advertising medium. Mail-order is a method of distribution in which a sale is initiated and completed through advertisements and return mail (or phone call). Mail-order is not an advertising medium, but it employs such advertising media as direct-mail, newspapers, magazines and radio in its selling effort.

WHO USES DIRECT-MAIL ADVERTISING?—Direct-mail advertising is so versatile that it is used at all market levels of the fashion industry to sell to prospective customers, active customers and inactive customers. It is used for trade, national and retail institutional and product objectives. It is used by retailers to bring in the business all by itself (this is called mail-order advertising) or to supplement the personal selling activity, or to bring customers to the point-of-sale. It is unique in mass media because it is *direct,* produced by the advertiser, and consequently does not have to compete with other ads for the customer's attention.

Direct-mail advertising is used by producers, manufacturers and retailers for the following:

1. To get mail orders.
2. To solicit inquiries from interested prospects, to be followed up by mail for their orders.
3. To help get "leads" for salespeople.
4. To follow up salespeople's calls.
5. To stimulate people to visit the point-of-sale or to see a specially planned demonstration, or other special event.
6. To keep in touch with active and inactive customers.
7. To tell customers of forthcoming sales events.

THE MAILING LIST—The audience for direct-mail advertising is based on a list of prospects to whom the advertisements are to be mailed. This list is generally not a prepared selection of names which can be purchased ready-made from mailing-list firms. Mailing-list firms are actually selling a service. This service is their ability to gather and classify names of various categories of customers. The ready-made lists they offer may have some value, but they are rarely selective enough to be effective. It is the responsibility of the *advertiser,* therefore, to determine just who his target audience is, and what part of this market he wishes on his list. After this has been determined, it is usually possible to develop this list himself much more effectively than anyone else could or would.

It should be apparent that the effectiveness of any direct-mail advertising is predetermined by the degree to which the people on the list are good prospects for the products advertised. What would it avail an advertiser to send booklets on expensive back-to-college clothes to customers who could not afford them, or for a fashion manufacturer to tell a small retailer the advantages of a quantity buying, or for a fabric shop to describe the "satisfaction of making your own clothes" to the woman who likes to buy her gowns in the most expensive metropolitan shops? The first demand of any direct-mail list is that it include only those who are in a position to use the product advertised.

HOW IS THE LIST DEVELOPED?—The direct opportunities for obtaining names of prospects are often so obvious that they are overlooked. Present and past customers usually form the best list for a direct-mail advertising program. Frequently a name will be on the customers' list when that person buys only occasionally, or buys little instead of much. Many businesses have developed effective mailing lists which have been used to convert inactive customers to active buyers.

Another excellent source of names is from the reports of salespeople. Many firms supply special forms for the salesperson to fill out. These forms provide information on active and prospective customers which help to classify them into categories based upon their special interests and requirements.

The mailing list can often be developed through direct mail designed for this purpose and through magazine, newspaper or radio advertisements which ask customers who are interested to write for further information and details.

## TELEVISION

Television is an advertising medium which offers the fashion advertiser some very special assets. In the lexicon of media sage Marshall McLuhan, it is the "coolest" of the media. McLuhan defines a cool medium as one with a high degree of audience involvement and participation. There seems to be very little question about the impact and appeal of a medium which can combine the most dramatic combinations of sight, sound, color and animation—and which is transmitted directly into the customer's own room.

The synergistic effect of two sensory stimuli, audio and visual, is regarded by psychologists to be a fundamental reason for the high degree of penetration which television commercials have attained. The creatively produced television commercial is unique in its ability to demonstrate the benefits and satisfactions of fashion products.

The appeal of attractive and interesting people saying and doing things with products comes very close to the effectiveness of good personal selling. Add to this appeal, the factor of entertainment which provides a virtually captive audience of huge proportion. This audience can be selectively designed by choosing certain programs and times of day or evening.

There is, therefore, hardly any argument about the assets of television in presenting a fashion message. Much of the drama and impact of a fashion show in "living color" is possible even in a thirty-second spot. The big problems are cost and expertise. The costs of creative production for television are beyond the know-how and finances of most stores. It is mainly the major retailer(s) in each community who are able to use television as a substantial part of their advertising effort. Some of these larger stores have utilized advertising agencies to plan, write, direct, film and produce the kind of commercials they would like their customers to see. Several of these stores have also added trained television practitioners to their sales promotion divisions. We see this as a trend, as there is every indication that the use of retail television is growing steadily—on the network level with such giant retailers as Sears and J.C. Penney, and on a local level with retailers of *all* sizes and descriptions.

## RADIO

Radio is an inescapable medium. There are more radios than people in the United States, according to the Radio Advertising Bureau. Over 7,000 stations with many different types of programming on AM and FM make this medium of the airways almost as ubiquitous as the air we breathe. Home sets, portables, plug-ins and car radios are among the little boxes that invade the daily lives of our people. Young people are reported to be sharply influenced by the correct choice of station by an advertiser, but radio listeners include every age group and different market segments within each age group. The radio advertiser has an opportunity to select a very personal target market by his choice of station, program and time of day.

This tremendous variety of choices and flexibility of timing enables the advertiser to take advantage of last-minute decisions to promote special offers to his customers. Radio advertising can be timely and current. It has a remarkable ability to appeal on an intimate level to customers. Its most effective use may be to attain institutional objectives. There are many excellent radio campaigns now being aired to create a strong image, build reputation, and develop identity for retailers. The lack of the sense of sight has not been a drawback in this respect. This is why radio is increasing at a very rapid rate as a medium for retail advertising. In the past radio and television may have been used by retailers to "back-up" newspaper advertising. This is changing and radio especially is being assigned a more important role in the retailer's media mix.

The National Retail Merchants Association (NRMA) has estimated that radio and television now constitute about 25 percent of retail advertising.

The special assets of radio as a retail advertising medium—*target audience selectivity* to reach the retailers most desired segments of the market; *intimacy* of the dialogue, the friendly radio voice (who often also reads the commercials), and familiar backgrounds of music add to its ability to appeal; *variety of programming* enables advertisers to sponsor programs or insert spots in a very flexible schedule which can increase and decrease in proportion to the sales objectives of the particular time; *companionship* of a radio is a media legend. A radio can go *anywhere* we go. Over 50 percent of the nation's adults, and 75 percent of our teenagers own portable radios. Radios are ever-present from shirt pockets to automobiles. It also provides the most comprehensive coverage of any medium. The entire population of this country could be considered the audience. The audience stays with radio through all seasons of the year; *timing* is less of a problem than in other media. Spots can be scheduled shortly before airing if necessary; CPM of radio has not escalated at the rate of competing media; *heavy frequency* of message is possible in a short time at a cost comparable to only a few newspaper or television advertisements. In some very small towns, radio is the only daily mass medium. It also does not have to compete with other ads at the time it is being aired. An example is the clutter of small ads on a single newspaper page, each competing for attention. Radio advertising does not have this problem. Its major asset is its selective coverage and its ability to get the kind of attention it wants from potential customers.

## THE MEDIA-MARKETING–
## MERCHANDISING CONNECTION

Fashion primary producers, apparel manufacturers, and fashion retailers are increasingly aware of the connection between their marketing and/or merchandising effort and media planning. This awareness is not confined to advertising agencies and communications practitioners.

The marketing manager, sales manager, merchandise manager, and sales promotion director are involved in media decisions. Those who are closest to the wants and needs of customers are needed by media planners for information and advice. The media department in an advertising agency has to have a considerable depth of knowledge in marketing and merchandising.

Marketing, merchandising, and promotion which rely on a structure of media planning can produce more from the advertising budget, sell more products, and enhance the reputation of the company. Firms on all the levels of the fashion industry now consider media planning a major consideration of marketing and merchandising management.

# 7

# The Creative Job of Putting Fashion Advertising Together

*Why* is an advertisement born? *What* are the various stages in its creation? *Who* decides *what* is to be advertised, *when, where* and *how* much for the advertisement? We will illustrate this entire procedure by tracing the life history of an advertisement from advertising plan to production.

## THE ADVERTISING PLAN

An advertising plan is a schedule for a prescribed period of time, from a year to a week, of the advertising that a firm intends to employ in order to attract business. Its format is usually that of a *planning calendar* with months, weeks and days designed to accommodate the necessary information. The advertising plan is formulated after the sales promotion appropriation and the sales promotion plan (discussed in Chapter 1) have been determined. It contains the following information:

1. Date on which advertisements will run
2. Divisions, departments, merchandise, services or ideas which will be advertised
3. Estimated sales of merchandise featured in *product* ads *(in the case of retailers)*

4. Media to be used
5. Amount of space to be used in each medium
6. Cost of space in dollars, (and *in the case of retailers,* as a percentage of sales)

The advertising plan should be flexible and permit revision upward or downward if necessary, should sales trends increase or decrease beyond or below expectation.

## TYPES OF ADVERTISING PLANS

The different types of plans used by firms in the fashion industry are as numerous as the different types of firms which exist. For purposes of clarity we will discuss advertising plans which have common characteristics regardless of whether we are considering primary, secondary or retail market levels. In other words, the following methods of developing advertising plans are basically similar for fashion primary producers and apparel manufacturers as well as retailers.

We shall consider two types of advertising plans:
1. The Whole-Firm Plan
2. The Divisional Plan

### THE WHOLE-FIRM PLAN

The planning of advertising is designed to consider objectives of the whole-firm as well as the product divisions of a producer or the merchandise divisions and departments of a retailer. When the objectives of the whole-firm are being discussed by top management (committees composed of administrative executives, product or merchandise managers, sales managers and promotion directors), there is no attempt to include individual product or departmental breakdowns. The *whole-firm* plan is viewed as a basis for the development of detailed *divisional plans* later on.

The whole-firm plan:
1. Establishes the product and institutional objectives for the firm for the period being planned;
2. Establishes the advertising allocation for the firm for this period;
3. Outlines the *major fashion themes and selling events* which may include all or several divisions or departments.

## THE DIVISIONAL PLAN

After top management has formulated the whole-firm plan they submit to the managers of each division and its departments, *divisional plans* which are schedules and budgets for advertising in selected media (newspapers, direct mail, radio . . .). Each plan will indicate:

1. The *advertising budget* for each class of media that the division is granted to aid in reaching its sales goals for the period.
2. The particular promotion, themes and selling events planned by the firm in which this division is expected to participate.

As each division head (in a retail store the merchandise manager) receives these budgets he uses the information to plan in detail the events and promotions which his division and its departments will undertake for the period.

These advertising plans also detail specifically:

1. Types of merchandise to be featured
2. Types of advertising activities to be employed
3. Price lines and conditions of sale
4. Preferred medium
5. Timing

Thus the individual divisional (and departmental) plans for advertising grow out of the whole-firm plan.

The sales promotion director and advertising manager receive the individual plans and coordinate these into a master advertising schedule for the entire store.

# ADVERTISING PROCEDURE FROM PLAN TO PRODUCTION

We can illustrate advertising procedure from plan to production by examining the procedure which initiates and produces a typical *retail* newspaper advertisement.

## BUYER'S PLAN FOR ADVERTISING

A store buyer will work with his divisional merchandise manager and the advertising manager to develop several weeks in advance his monthly plan for advertising. (We referred to this previously in the case of retailers as the department plan.) This plan will include:

- Descriptions of ads to be run
- Items to be featured
- Prices
- Estimated dollar sales of the advertised merchandise
- The size and cost of the ad
- The medium
- The day of publication

After the divisional merchandise manager has coordinated the individual departmental plans, the divisional plan is submitted to the general merchandise manager, the sales promotion director, and advertising manager for approval and integration into a *store* (whole-firm) *advertising schedule.*

## BUYER'S INFORMATION FORM

The buyer knows he has an ad coming up by referring to the approved advertising schedule usually a week to ten days before publication. He then fills out a Buyer's Information Form ("advertising request form," "advertising copy information," are other terms for the same type of form). It is essential that information for product advertising* originate with the buyer. The buyer knows the needs and wants of his customers better than anyone. He buys the merchandise and knows its selling points and appeals. He is best equipped to tell customers what satisfactions they will derive from the purchase of these items. He has the major responsibility for selling the merchandise quickly, at a profit. He should be the most concerned with the creation of an effective ad.

The buyer's information form in addition to necessary factual information, should contain all of the aforementioned buyer's reasons for buying, and most important, the customer's reasons for wanting the products involved. If a buyer neglects to include sufficient information of this nature, copywriters may not bother to "dig," but will use whatever facts are available. This type of copy is often written by "formula" and lacks the customer's point-of-view. It may not attain sales objectives. Figure 39 is a typical Buyer's Information Form which is used by buyers in a major department store.

---

*Product advertising includes regular-price-line ads, special price and clearance ads —as differentiated from *institutional* advertising which is usually not initiated by the buyer.

# BUYER'S INFORMATION FOR ADVERTISING

(Must be accompanied by merchandise samples)

## Important selling features

List in order of importance the selling features (and benefits to the consumer) that you consider the most important reason why the customer should buy this merchandise. Tell us why this merchandise is superior to similar offerings she may have seen.

Be specific. Do not attempt to write the copy, but indicate clearly, and in your own terms, the reasons why YOU bought this particular merchandise. Given this information, we will endeavor to translate it into an enthusiastic and persuasive advertisement aimed at convincing the customer that this is merchandise she needs, wants and should buy.

Please do NOT list price or savings here (use box at right).

1. _____ (Main Feature)
2. _____
3. _____
4. _____
5. _____
6. _____
7. _____
8. _____
9. _____
10. _____

(If necessary, use other side for additional information)

Have you included MATERIAL? FIBER CONTENT? WASHABILITY? SIZES? COLORS? NO-IRON? FINISHES? FAMOUS BRANDS?

_____ (Data)

Dept. No. _____
Day of week _____
Date _____
Paper _____
Linage _____ $
☐ This is a repeat ad.
See _____ (pages) _____ (date)
For copy _____ Art _____
General approach _____
☐ This offering should be keyed for selling starting on _____ (day of week)

☐ REQUEST FOR NEW ARTWORK
List number of illustrations required, indicating item to be featured, if any.
_____
_____
_____
Detailed information regarding artwork must be attached to merchandise samples. (Use Form X3A-5)

☐ There is a vendor allowance in connection with this advertisement in the amount of $ _____
Fill out, sign and attach BUYER'S REQUEST FOR PAID ADVERTISEMENT here.

## PRICE
_____ each, _____ pair, _____ set
☐ I have requested a comparative price and I have sent copy of this form together with samples to the Comparison Office.
regularly _____ usually _____
formerly _____ originally _____
manufacturer's list price _____

## MAIL AND PHONE SOLICITATION
☐ Mail and phone orders filled within 5 days of receipt of order.
☐ Mail and phone orders filled on or more.
☐ Mail and phone orders filled while quantities last.
☐ No mail or phone orders.

## SHIPPING CHARGES
☐ Beyond motor delivery area add $_____ handling.
☐ For each additional unit add only $_____ for handling.
☐ Beyond motor delivery area, express charges will be collected on delivery.
☐ Plus small charge for home delivery.

## CREDIT
☐ THIS OFFERING WILL BE SOLD ON CREDIT. ONLY $_____ DOWN, MONTHS TO PAY.

## BRANCH PARTICIPATION
☐ ALSO AT HEMPSTEAD   ☐ ALSO AT BARTON
☐ ALSO AT GARDEN CITY   ☐ BROOKLYN STORE ONLY

*Figure 39. A typical buyer's information form.*

110

## THE COMPARISON OFFICE

The buyer's information form in many stores is made out in triplicate. The buyer keeps the third copy. He sends the original form to his divisional merchandise manager for authorization. The original and second copy are sent to the *comparison shopping department* along with samples of the merchandise. This is part of the system to insure comparative shopping in competitive stores of the to-be-advertised merchandise. The original form is sent to the advertising department after the comparison office has verified that the merchandise has been, or will be shopped before publication of the ad.

Though the comparison office is mentioned here, it is well to note that relatively few stores have such a department. The value of a comparison office is enormous, but many stores cannot afford this luxury. With the strong advances of consumerism and consumer education, knowledge of a store's specific target market is most important. Merchandisers and advertisers *must* know what their customers know.

It is usually the buyer's responsibility to shop, or to have an assistant buyer shop and report on the competition. The other stores' themes, promotional events, prices and assortments must be observed. It is well to keep in mind the attitude of most consumers: Merchandise need not be identical. Equivalent merchandise and similar items of equal quality and performance may qualify as substitutes to a consumer.

It is foolish to advertise a "special price" when the same or equivalent merchandise is around town or at one competitor's store at the same or at a lower price. Your offer is not then so "special." Careless promotions can destroy or impair the confidence of customers.

If the merchandise you offer has one or more points of superiority or difference, selling points which have meaning to the consumer, it is important to mention these points of difference in your ad. Only a careful check of the competition can reveal the facts of your claim.

Furthermore, a comparison shopping last week or last month is of little value. The checkup must be made immediately prior to running your ad. Markets move swiftly. Though some stores choose to ignore competitive prices, it is wise to be aware of what the competition is offering.

*The buyer confers with the merchandising manager.*

*Advertisement planning meeting between the buyer, merchandise manager and advertising director.*

*Copywriter develops copy appeals and approaches from Buyer's Information Form and merchandise sample.*

*Layouts are started by art department based on copy, buyer's information and merchandise.*

*The art department creates illustrations and/or photography according to the layout.*

*Advertising production pastes up all elements into a mechanical for plate-making printing production.*

112

*Proofs are checked by art department and the buyer.*

*The customer sees the ad in the local newspaper.*

*Figure 40. Advertising Procedure—From Plan to Production*

### PUTTING THE AD "IN WORK"

The advertising manager checks the buyer's information form against the advertising schedule and puts the advertisement into production. He starts by conferring with his copy chief and art director to determine the most effective manner of presenting the sales message. The discussion continues until an exchange of viewpoints and suggestions produces ideas for copy, layout and art. In many stores, the advertising manager will do a *rough preliminary layout* to indicate to his staff his ideas for the ad. This layout can include headline and text copy suggestions from the copy chief. Now the advertising department staff can put the ad "in work."

### COPY

The copywriter receives the approved information form plus the rough layout and copy suggestions. Copy is the "thinking behind the ad" and is largely responsible for the layout design and art which will be used to interpret it. The sales message to the customer comes from sales objectives and appeals supplied to the copywriter by the buyer in the information form. The copywriter has the rough layout, copy suggestions and the buyer's thinking, as ammunition in creating a persuasive advertisement which can be dramatically *visualized.* The copywriter must therefore think in terms of how his copy will *look,* how it can be translated into finished layout and art for maximum effectiveness.

## LAYOUT

The final copy with all its components—headline, subhead, text, description, prices, slogans, logos, and other design-identity details—is sent to the buyer for suggestions and approval. After the necessary revisions and approval are obtained, copy and rough layout are given to a layout artist who does a finished or *comprehensive layout*. This layout indicates very clearly what the actual advertisement will look like. In the comprehensive layout, all elements are exactly in place and artwork is drawn to carefully simulate the photography and/or illustrations which will be used. Figure 40 is an illustration of the procedure up to this point.

## ADVERTISING PRODUCTION

The advertising manager who is responsible for the overall quality of the advertisement checks the comprehensive layout and may (depending upon store policy) show it to the buyer. Once approved, an artist and/or photographer is assigned to execute the illustrations and/or photographs, as indicated by the layout.

At the same time the *advertising production* staff is working with a duplicate of the layout. They will do a typographical layout to indicate the *size* and *style* of type, (following the typographical styles pre-established for the store), borders and other design elements which will be used in the ad.

## PRINTING PRODUCTION

The finished art is sent to the buyer for approval. If it is approved the art is "sized" or marked for reduction to fit the layout. Additional instructions are sent to photoengravers as to the manner in which the photoengravings or plates are to be finished. See Figure 41 for an illustrated explanation of the photoengraving principles of making plates. This is delivered with the copy layout and typographical layout to the *newspaper* for reproduction and first proofs. The newspaper completes the advertising promotion process by preparing the elements of the advertisement for *printing production.* This is done by first making photoengravings of illustrations or photography (if these have not been produced by the store). Then typographers set type according to the typographical layout. The photoengravings and type are then arranged exactly as in the layout. Then the first proofs of the ad are pulled on a proof press.

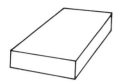

Suppose you had a flat piece of work . . .

. . . and passed a roller of ink across it . . .

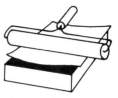

. . . and pressed paper against it.

The paper would come out like this.

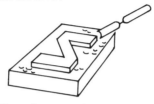

Now if you marked the letter "Z" and carved away the rest of the wood, leaving the "Z" raised . . .

. . . and passed an inked roller over the wood . . .

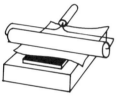

. . . then pressed a piece of paper against the wood . . .

. . . the paper would bear this imprint.

We begin again. This time we want to reproduce the letter "T."

It is photographed on a metal surface coated with photographic emulsion.

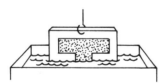

To make the "T" stand out, the metal surrounding it is etched away chemically instead of by a tool.

The result is also a raised letter.

Then if you passed an inked roller over it . . .

. . . and pressed paper against it . . .

. . . you will have printed the "T" on paper. Print as many as you want.

Figure 41. The photoengraving principle of making plates.

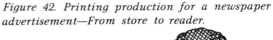

*Figure 42. Printing production for a newspaper advertisement—From store to reader.*

**A**

*The store's advertising department sends photoengravings, layout and copy to the newspaper advertising department manager.*

**B**

*The newspaper ad manager "deals" it out to a member of his production staff who prepares it for typography.*

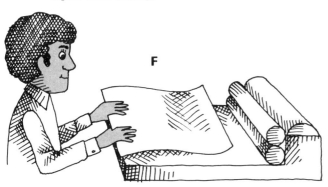

**F**

*First proofs of the ad are pulled on a proof press . . .*

**G**

*. . . And sent to the store's advertising department for OK—The production manager and the buyer get copies for approval and necessary revisions.*

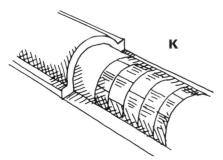

**K**

*A curved metal casting or page stereotype is then cast from the ad mat.*

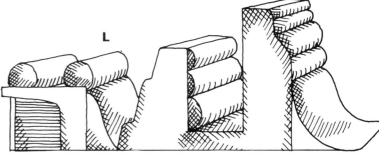

**L**

*All page stereotypes are put on rotary letterpresses.*

116

*The copy is set in type.*

*A proof is proofread with the copy.*

*Photoengravings and type are arranged exactly as in the layout.*

*Corrected proofs are sent back to the newspaper.*

*Corrections are made . . . and a new set of revised proofs are sent to the store's advertising department and buyer for final OK.*

*A mold in heavy "cardboard" (Newspaper Ad Mat) is made under pressure at the steam table from the chase.*

*The printed papers are hurried to distribution points . . .*

*. . . and to the customer.*

117

The newspaper completes the advertising production* process by sending these proofs to the store's advertising department. The advertising manager dispatches one copy to the buyer and two other copies to his art and production departments. Each is responsible for their respective revisions and corrections of reproduction, placement or content. Once these are made, corrected proofs are sent back to the newspaper. A new set of *revised proofs* is pulled and submitted to the store for final approval. The advertisement is now ready for its scheduled publication. Figure 42 is an illustration of the advertising production process.

The entire process we have just described could possibly be done in two days. But this would be a teeth-chattering emergency schedule, not conducive to effective quality. Most stores operate within a five to eight day *schedule* (working days). (See Figure 40.)

## THE ELEMENTS OF PRINT ADVERTISEMENTS FOR NEWSPAPERS, MAGAZINES AND DIRECT MAIL

What is a print advertisement made of? It has been called salesmanship in print." The elements of which this salesmanship is composed are as follows:
1. Copy
2. Art (Photography or Illustrations)
3. White Space

### COPY

All print advertisements start with a blank white space. The size of this space is determined by the dimensions of the ad. The first element which goes into this white space is copy. *Copy* is the means by which the advertiser's selling objectives are made articulate to the reader. No matter how long or short, we shall refer to copy as all the reading matter in an advertisement. Advertising copy has components which includes *headline, subhead, text* or *body* copy and the advertiser's signature *(logotype)* and *slogans* (Figure 43). Each of the *components of copy* has a job to do.

---

*The *advertising production procedure* varies tremendously according to medium and method of printing used. The process described here is representative only of *newspaper* advertising production for newspapers which use *rotary letterpress.*

118

*Figure 43. The components of copy in a print ad. Text (or Body Copy) may have four parts: (1) Amplification of* HEAD *and* SUBHEAD; *(2) further selling points and sub-appeals; (3) evidence or proof; (4) closing.*

HEADLINES—Headlines should be written to *attract attention* and work with the visual to develop reader *interest*. Many copywriters feel that the most effective headlines contain the main appeal (keynote) and/or selling points which would be the most powerful reason(s) for the reader to respond to the sales message. Many copywriters also feel that brand names and institutions should be frequently mentioned in headlines.

These are the different types of headlines each with its own approach:

1. *News* or *Factual* (Almost like a news article)
2. *Curiosity* or *Provocative* (Often is a question "What does *your* wardrobe say . . . ?")
3. *Selective* (Mentions the target customer "Women over 40 . . .")
4. *Narrative* (A slice of life—a story, often with dialogue)
5. *Label* (Most used in fashion advertising "The vested suit.")
6. *Advice* and *Promise* (The most projective "You'll have better skin in 10 days . . .")
7. *Command* (The hard sell "Supplies are limited—don't delay . . .")

SUBHEADS (SUBHEADLINES)—Subheads are used when head-lines need further explanation or there is a need to add further appeals and/or selling points. A good example is in the use of a provocative headline such as "On Your Way to $35,000 A Year?" and a subhead "It might be the *Stanley Blacker* you wear." The subhead is often a connector between headline and text.

TEXT OR BODY COPY—Text is used to lead into an amplification of headline and connect to its idea. It attempts to stimulate a *desire* for the product (or response to ideas) by *adding selling points* of superiority or uniqueness; offering *evidence and proof* to support initial claims; adding *sub-appeals* to the main appeal; and asking for reader action by closing the message. The closing can be very soft sell and implied, or hard sell and commanding, depending upon the approach and "tone" of the ad.

SLOGANS—Slogans are *repeated* selling points or appeals which are of prime importance to a product, brand or institution. The slogan must sound as well as it reads, be memorable and bear repetition in all of the firm's advertising. Bloomingdale's, New York, emphasized its fashion authority and prominence as a retailer with— "Like No Other Store In The World."

LOGOS (LOGOTYPE)—Logos are engravings or type bearing the signature or name, trademark or graphic symbol of a company or store. The Macy's red star is a long-running example. In broadcast media this could be a musical or sound effects signature.

### HOW CLEVER SHOULD FASHION COPY BE?

Regardless of the specific objectives of an ad, its ultimate purpose is to stimulate response, generate sales and create impressions. The copywriter's job is to put together the right combination of words which will attract the reader's *Attention;* arouse his *Interest* in the message; create *Desire* for products and ideas; stimulate *Action* awareness or response. The selling process (AIDA*) is evident here as it will be in other sales promotion activities.

*A-I-D-A is a mnemonic used to describe *effective selling procedure.* The steps are A: attracting attention; I: arousing interest; D: creating desire; A: stimulating action. In personal selling we can add S: insuring satisfaction.

Customers are exposed to great variations in copy in newspapers, magazines and direct mail. Some copy may tempt customers to take immediate action and other copy may fail—even when they are good prospects for the product. Why does one piece of copy sell the customer while another does not register at all?

If we could put this answer into a formula there would be no need for research into customer wants and needs. Copywriting is a unique skill which is developed by writers who study fundamental characteristics and behavior (demographic and psychographic) of their customers. They examine and develop unique selling points and compelling appeals about their product. They familiarize themselves with characteristics of media and its audiences. They are aware of the techniques of layout, visualization and illustration to make their copy come to life. The copywriter should have a visual concept of his ideas which will enable him to work with an art director to create the most emphatic visual and verbal message.

A guideline for all copy today is believability. The copy must have compelling style to be seen and read—but believability *sells.* Cleverness and glamourization in fashion advertising is admired by many readers, and generally enjoyed by members of the advertising fraternity, until it goes beyond belief.

The hard-headed businessman will often appreciate a clever advertisement, but he measures success by results. Neither the clever quip nor the immediate response is always entirely ideal. Great advertising does not always bring immediate results, and great advertising is not necessarily clever.

Young aspiring copywriters often strive frantically for clever copy. Nothing could be more frustrating to the objectives of the neophyte copywriter than a constant effort to be clever. What is the answer then to the question, *How clever should fashion advertising be?*

There is no simple formula to answer this question, but there are tested techniques that have produced favorable results over many years of observation of thousands of ads and hundreds of campaigns. And there are always new and untested techniques to be explored. First, let us establish that if an advertiser says something in his advertising often enough and for long enough, it gets to be known, if not liked. Possibly the most annoying campaign ever to be employed was the whining brat who blanketed radio airwaves with a call for "More Park Sausages, Mom!" But until he came up with his insistent and monotonous demand for Park, it was by no means a particularly well-known brand. The factory where these sausages are made now has the entire quotation on the sign over the plant instead of just the name of the company. An interesting note on an advertiser's awareness of customer attitudes was the more recent version of the Park Sausage commercial . . . Consumers who complained about this fresh kid now hear him call—"More Park Sausages, Mom—*please?*"

And so we have the annoying repetitious copy which admittedly has an excellent factor or remembrance. But this is not what people refer to when they speak of clever copy. A fashion headline that gets attention and stimulates the reader or listener to further interest in the message may not be clever, but it serves the principal objective of a headline. The message in a headline should be "Read me . . . and read what follows me." Such a headline steals attention away from its competition. Now, clever or not, it achieves its objective. The important point to realize is that cleverness is not the ultimate aim of good advertising. Clarity is! Believability is!

Listeners and viewers often write bitter letters of objection to companies who use annoying advertising, but it seems that for every objector, there must be legions of buyers. It is common knowledge that dentists do not recommend chewing gum. Nevertheless, one manufacturer insists that his brand is recommended by ". . . four out of five dentists." Wrigley, another manufacturer had the effrontery to advise in a campaign that chewing will make work seem lighter. Though this is not exactly believable, it sold chewing gum.

Writing fashion copy requires a unique sense of the dramatic. Not everyone is capable of this. The fashion copywriter must be conversant with the most current fashion trends, popular designers, styles, fabrics and colors. A depth of product knowledge, including stages and levels of merchandise-acceptance is also required. An expert fashion writer understands historical fashion cycles and the reappearance of styles and "looks." The copywriter is an observer of consumer behavior and understands the nature of the specific motivations and desire for fashion. It is also vital for a fashion copywriter to have the appreciation of, and a feeling of having worn dramatic and exciting styles. Fashion has a mystique all its own— it is illusion and fantasy and its writing must reflect this. The most successful fashion copy is a judicious blend of the romantic and the factual, for the consumer is also interested in colors, sizes, quality features, performance, cleaning care, and price. The copy, above all, should be person-to-person, intimate and lively. The fashion copywriter must consider all of the above in the context of the product.

The language of fashion should change to accommodate the product. Price is handled more subtly (or left out completely) in exclusive fashion advertising. Volume fashion could be less imaginative and emotional, and more practical and factual, handling its drama in a somewhat lower key. Fashion copy on all levels must use words effectively and concisely. The message should come through quickly and work with dramatic photography and fashion illustrations without detracting from them.

If the message of the ad is perfectly clear, and sufficient, numbers of people are stimulated to take action; clever or not, the ad has served its purpose. Blunt honesty in advertising seems to be the most elusive, most desirable, most surprising, and most effective of all devices and techniques in advertising. When the advertising agency Doyle, Dane, Bernbach was faced with the problem of advertising the Volkswagen, they made it clear in their advertising that this was an "ugly" little car with a great many advantages. The advertiser captured the imagination of the public and made ownership of a Volkswagen a matter of status.

When advertising is completely believable, the message comes through without the doubts that so much advertising gets and deserves. Fantasy has become so much a part of fashion advertising where the reader or listener is promised happiness, gift-wrapped. There is no need to deny that the public has responded in the past with great gullibility to these advertised promises of hitherto unattainable glories of glamour. Ask any cosmetic manufacturer about the best way to sell . . . let us say, common cold cream. There are creams to make women soft, charming, glowing, elegant, sophisticated, desirable, young (regardless of age), tender, regal . . . and if you chose, a long list may be added to these adjectives which are used in the promotion of the common cold cream. Is this an evil pursuit? According to several writers on the subject of advertising, this appeal to the emotions is not accepted as honorable.

Where does one draw the line between honesty and misrepresentation? Truly, an appeal to emotions is not in itself dishonest. A misrepresentation of facts, exaggerations, promises of fantasy beyond all imagination is pure dishonesty. The public is beginning to be aware of such dishonesty and only deliverable benefits should be advertised. The great problem is that too few copywriters research their product benefits and instead let their imaginations and profit motives dictate the copy. This is especially regrettable when product advantages are there, but no one has taken the time or effort to search them out and then to write the copy.

Hammacher Schlemmer, a New York shop that specializes in unusual items, has several times advertised a box that does nothing, holds nothing and is nothing. They sell to people who are seeking gag items to give friends who "have everything." The important point is that the store advertises the item as having absolutely no advantage or use. It is probably the most useless item that has ever been manufactured and sold on exactly those terms. That is truth in advertising.

There is no crime in adding glamour to merchandise when it is advertised, if there is no misrepresentation. Glamour, color and imagination are as much a part of life as fact, character and heart-beat.

Cleverness does not cross the lines of honesty. An advertisement can be clever *and* honest. In fact, as pointed out in a previous Volkswagen campaign, the utter honesty of the copy is the heart of its cleverness. When Volkswagen introduced their van, it was called a "box on wheels." This was an honest description of its appearance. Then, the copy went on to enumerate the many advantages of the "box."

Then what is the answer to cleverness and to attention-getting advertising? How does the advertiser develop clever copy? Basically, the primary route to cleverness is a full, thorough and penetrating research—knowledge of product, of market, of competition, of publics, of public interests and attitudes. These factors are the absolute necessity for consistently clever advertising. Without these elements, the copywriter has no way of knowing what his public will think of as "clever." What a corps of copywriters considers as clever can be a colossal flop to the audience to whom the copy is directed. Advertising is clever only when customers in appreciable numbers consider it so. Clarity and delivery of the message must come first. If cleverness does not fog a message, then there is room to be clever.

## WHAT THE COPYWRITER SHOULD KNOW BEFORE HE WRITES

1. Complete knowledge of the product or service to be advertised, and the outstanding features from the viewpoint of the customer.
2. The features of and claims made by the competition. This knowledge can suggest the points of difference he should include in his own copy.
3. The copy strategy of the ad. What is the advertiser's purposes in running this ad—immediate and long range?
4. The copy platform. Good copy has organization, clarity, conciseness and unity. It proceeds in a logical fashion to state its appeals and selling points and then close. The writer's thoughts should be developed without confusion, extraneous matter, catch phrases or ideas not pertinent to the *"big idea"* or "unique selling proposition," benefit or feature which will best sell the product.
5. The editorial style of the publication. The skillful copywriter tries to make his ad an integral part of the medium being used. The medium's editorial or programming content sets the tone for his copy.
6. The response desired. The copywriter must know beforehand what to ask the reader to do. The advertiser wants to sell his product—but shall the copy ask the reader to decide now, consider it at her leisure, or ask to see the product the next time she is at the dealer?

The copywriter who practices his art intelligently realizes that the customer is the most influential element in copy. The feelings and preferences of the users of the product determine selection of the appeals and determine the approach of copy. The copywriter regards his reader, viewer, or listener as a human being and not as a mechanical responder to a hard-sell pitch.

## ART

In advertising, "One picture is *not always* worth a thousand words" —but the inclusion of a compelling *visual* (photograph or illustration) in an ad can be a vital factor in determining its effectiveness.

An effective illustration helps to select the audience for an advertisement. It assists the copy to portray how problems are solved and satisfactions realized from the use of a product. It pictures happy solutions, describes features and establishes identity. Illustrations generate future recognition at the point-of-sale for the benefits which a purchase would bring.

Customers have become more and more picture-conscious. This as a result of the movies, tabloid newspapers, photo magazines, picture books and television. We communicate in mass media through the visual. People want to *see.* Today, the camera goes everywhere to see for us.

The value of the visual in fashion advertising cannot be overrated. Certainly those ads which are *seen and read* are most effective. In most advertising it is very unusual for anything but the simplest sales message to be carried by a picture alone. But, in a fashion ad the photograph or illustration can have a larger share in its success than in other product areas. The picture works to attract attention, and relates to copy designed to stimulate customer motivation. The use of purely attention-getting illustration in an ad is generally too obvious to the reader. The most effective ad uses illustration to serve the sales objective, appeals and approach of the ad. A fashion illustration or photograph which can attract the eye, create a mood, and then make the attributes of the style more desirable is helping to sell. The experienced art director knows the types of illustration and photography which will attract certain audiences. It is his job to create dramatic visualizations which show how merchandise is used to satisfy the wants of the customer. Fashion illustrations can show what products will do for the reader in the environment which the customer would like to find himself. A skilled artist or photographer can dramatize fashion merchandise in its most advantageous perspective and in its most attractive setting.

The three major types of art used in fashion advertising, *line drawings, wash illustration, photography,* are illustrated in Figures 44 and 45.

## FASHION ILLUSTRATION VS. PHOTOGRAPHY

Both photography and wash illustration have advantages and disadvantages as art in fashion advertisements. Newspapers use methods of printing and paper which are inferior to the reproduction techniques and paper used by magazines.

126

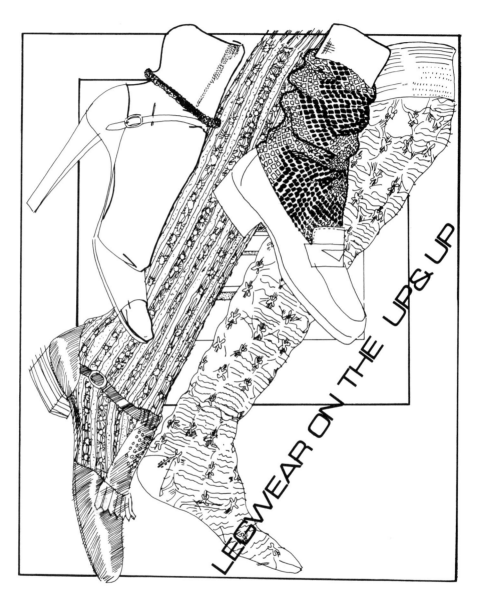

Figure 44. Line Drawings: Composed of black lines, solid masses and "cross-hatch" lines to simulate shaded or halftone areas. (Courtesy of WWD. Illustration by Catherine Clayton Purnell.)

*Figure 45. Photography and Wash Illustration. (Courtesy of WWD. Illustration by Catherine Clayton Purnell and photos by Lynn Karlin.)*

This is why photography does not reproduce as well in newspapers as it does in magazines. Halftones (photoengravings made from photographs or wash illustrations, rather than line drawings) will not reproduce as well as photoengravings made from line drawings. Some retailers will use fashion wash illustrations which produce halftones that are better adapted to the rapid printing techniques and comparatively low quality paper (newsprint) used by newspapers.

The fashion photograph can be used in newspapers but it requires special retouching and handling with still no guarantee of good reproduction. Compare the quality of wash illustrations and photographs in your newspaper. See which is clearer and shows more detail. Notice how many retailers now use fashion photography for dramatic mood, and line drawings for selling point details.

Photography may not be as "kind" to fashion merchandise as the artist's interpretation. The cost of good, flattering photography plus fees for professional models are prohibitive to many retailers. The fashion photograph is at its best in magazines and newspaper supplements (printed through different techniques and on higher quality paper than the regular run-of-the-paper, ROP). Photography has a realism and a news interest which makes it highly desirable to magazine advertisers where the budget for each ad is adequate to cover its higher costs. The dramatic true-to-life impact of good fashion photography is a mainstay in national advertising done by fashion producers and apparel manufacturers. Magazine ads also use line drawings and wash illustrations but to a more limited degree.

## PICTORIAL AND SYMBOLIC ILLUSTRATION

All illustration is characterized as either *pictorial* or *symbolic*. Pictorial or descriptive illustration portrays merchandise in true-to-life fashion so customers can see how a product looks and may be used. When this is accompanied by clear, persuasive copy, customers can make up their minds to purchase by merely *seeing* and *reading* the advertisement. In advertising which seeks immediate sales, the pictorial illustration is most important.

Symbolic or decorative illustration is fundamentally impressionistic in character. It seeks to create a mood or atmosphere. It may suggest the primary nature of the merchandise but it leaves details to the reader's imagination. Symbolic illustration may also be so abstract as to only hint at some feature of the product or its derivation. In the chapter on display you will see that window display can also use alternatives that are either pictorial or symbolic (abstract).

## WHITE SPACE

When you decide to run a print advertisement, one of the first decisions you must make is: How much space? How much you buy from a print advertising medium for your ad is the white space you will have as a physical element. The division of this space will be a determining factor in the ad being noticed and read. The space in the advertisement which is unoccupied by copy or art gives emphasis and contrast to the design. We refer to this as the white space in the advertisement. The dividing of space is accomplished by the particular arrangement of copy and art elements within the dimensions of an ad. The working diagram of this arrangement is called *layout**.

## LAYOUT

Layout is an arrangement of physical elements of copy, art and the division of white space within the boundaries of an advertisement.

The function of a layout is to provide a "blueprint" in which the elements are placed and sized. Layout can help art and copy do their selling job more effectively in the following ways.

DISTINCTIVENESS—Through techniques which involve unique uses of white space, visuals, perspective, color, proportion and balance, the layout can give advertising an identity which is recognized by the customer. The ad which pleases the reader by virtue of its attractive design is more likely to be read.

GAZE MOTION—The arrangement of elements in an ad can guide the eye by offering a visual path for it to follow. This helps assure that important elements are noticed and read.

EMPHASIS—Layout can arrange elements so that some are empha-

*In the case of direct-mail advertisement, the layout is usually worked on a blank dummy of the circular booklet, pages of catalog, etc.

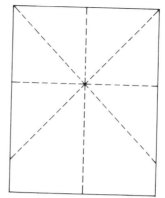

*Figure 46. Indicates the various dividing lines of an ad: horizontal, vertical, and diagonals. When the copy and art elements are symmetrically arranged in equal weight on both sides of these various dividing lines, the ad is in formal balance. When the arrangement is asymmetrical, the ad is informally balanced.*

sized over others. By attracting added attention to certain parts of copy, it is possible to present a stronger appeal to the customer.

BALANCE—An attribute of good design is balanced structure. Good design has a stability which makes it attractive to look at. The layout artist attempts to balance various sizes and shapes of copy and art to achieve *clarity, harmony* and *unity* in his design. Balance in a layout means that both halves of an advertisement have the same characteristics of power (e.g., the power or weight of an element is determined by its size, shape, intensity or color).

From an optical viewpoint, an ad is divided at a point about five-eighths of the way up the page. It is this optical center which the eye invariably chooses on a printed page. Figure 46 indicates the various dividing lines of an ad: horizontal, vertical and diagonals. When the copy and art elements are symmetrically arranged in equal weight on both sides of these various dividing lines the ad is in *formal balance.* When the arrangement is asymmetrical the ad is *informally balanced.* (See Figure 47.)

Formal balance as the term implies is more static to the eye. Informal balance has more gaze motion, and this presents a more dynamic effect.

*Figure 47. Formal vs. Informal*

## ADVERTISING PRODUCTION

The process of preparing an advertisement for printing reproduction is called advertising production. It involves the "pasting-up" on art board, elements of art and copy into position designated by the layout. The finished ad is called a "paste-up" or *mechanical.* The production department has the responsibility for effective translation of copy and art into *print.* The copy must be converted into *type.* The art (illustration or photograph) is processed into *photoengravings* or whatever other vehicle is needed for the particular printing process being employed. Advertising production is usually under the direction of the art director who is a skilled judge of design, proportion, color and reproduction. The art director has the responsibility for the advertisement's physical appearance, its design and its effectiveness in interpreting the sales message in the copy.

The three major printing processes are: *Letterpress, Offset Lithography* and *Gravure* (Intaglio).

132

LETTERPRESS PRINTING —Letterpress printing is still the major technique used by newspapers. It is printing from letters, lines and halftone dots raised above the surface of the metal (type and photo-engravings). In Figure 48 sketches A and B show the basic principle of letterpress printing. Sketches C and D show letterpresses; one a *flat-bed cylinder,* and the other a *rotary press* (such as those which print newspapers).

OFFSET LITHOGRAPHY—Offset lithography is printing from a smooth surface. It is used by many magazines, and is rapidly replacing letterpress in the printing of newspapers (utilizing presses specifically geared to the printing of newsprint). Figure 49, sketches A and B show the basic principle of offset lithography.

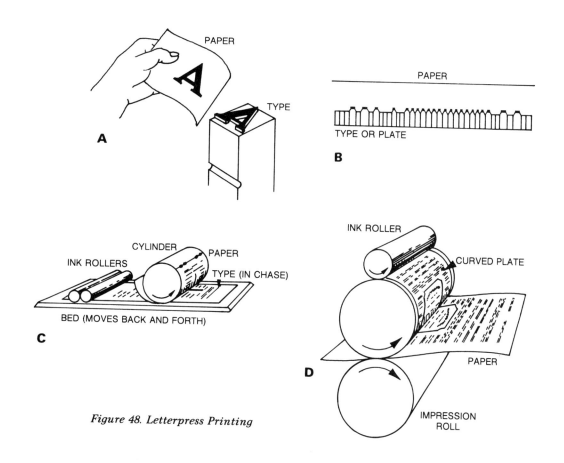

*Figure 48. Letterpress Printing*

133

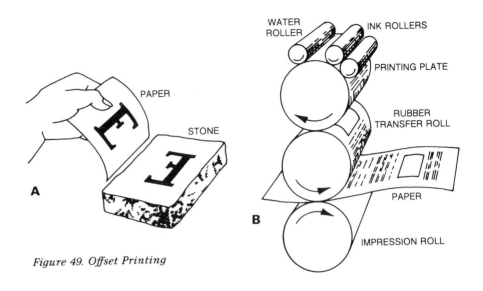

Figure 49. Offset Printing

GRAVURE PRINTING (INTAGLIO)—Gravure printing is printing from letters, lines and halftone dots cut into or etched out of metal plates. It is used by very fine fashion magazines, and quality publications for excellent color reproduction. *Rotogravure* is used in several magazine supplements in Sunday newspapers such as *The New York Times Magazine.* Figure 50, sketches A, B, and C show the gravure principle.

Figure 50. Gravure Printing (Intaglio)

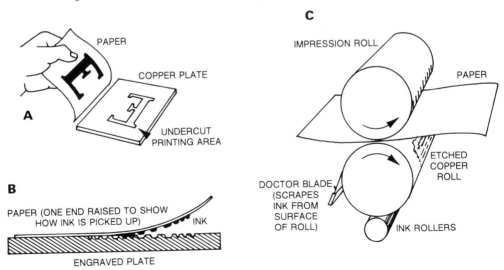

# THE ELEMENTS OF COMMERCIALS
# FOR RADIO AND TELEVISION

## RADIO

A prime consideration in the creation and production of radio commercials is the need to custom-design the message for a very selective target audience. Radio commercials cannot fire "buckshot"—they must take careful aim on a target group. They should be brief —even a 60-second commercial is limited to about 125 words.

The commercial should be of a quality needed to "get the message across." It is not difficult to prepare and produce spot commercials in a short time and a very low budget. But it is not wise. Good radio commercials often need more time and money to produce than ads in newspapers and magazines.

A commercial which is poorly conceived and executed can turn radio sets off. The radio commercial (as in television) is an "interrupter"—it stops the news, music or conversation. If it annoys the listener because of its poor quality—it can hardly be expected to sell.

Radio commercials can consist of announcements which are read from scripts or taped in advance (see Figure 51). The commercial can be read by a radio personality, station announcer, disc jockey, news commentator or by the advertiser himself. Professional actors can be used for more-than-one-voice dialogues designed to simulate reality. These should never be done "live."

NARRATIVE DRAMATIZATIONS—These can give a "slice-of-life" in sequences which require professional actors and sophisticated music background and sound effects. Narrative dramatizations can demonstrate the use of products with vivid visualizations in sound.

SINGING AND MUSICAL COMMERCIALS—These are attention-getters often used at both ends of the spot. Singing and musical commercials are expensive to produce and can be irritating if the techniques are amateurish. Some of the music being written for radio and television commercials is better then some of the popular music being written.

HUMOR—In commercials, humor is very popular and helps to counteract the intrusive effect. There have been many commercials

```
CLIENT:  Montaldo's                          LENGTH:   30 sec.

PRODUCT:  The "Two-Eighteen" Shop

AGENCY:  Emerson/Wilson, Inc.


TITLE:  "Lunch and Fashion"
```

MONTALDO THEME

FADE MUSIC UNDER SFX OF LUNCH CONVERSATION, ANIMATED WOMEN'S VOICES, TINKLING

OF GLASSES, ETC.

|  | ANNCR: |
|---|---|
|  | Nobody really has lunch at Tiffany's...But lunch at |
|  | Montaldo's is for real...It's for the career girl... |
| SFX:  LUNCH, VOICES, ETC. | Every Thursday from noon 'til one-thirty.  You can enjoy |
|  | lunch for a dollar and see informal modeling.  It will |
|  | show you what the Two-Eighteen Shop is all about...A |
|  | special place where you'll find clothes that carry the |
|  | look of quality and fashion.  All designed and priced |
| MUSIC UP-- DELIGHTED VOICES, APPLAUSE. | with the career girl in mind.  Enjoy.  Montaldo's lunch |
|  | special every Thursday, anytime between noon and one-thirty. |
|  | Montaldo's Two-Eighteen Shop--Uptown |

*Figure 51. A script for a radio commercial which serves the same function as a print advertisement layout. (Courtesy of RAB, Radio Advertising Bureau.)*

both on radio and television which were so humorous and entertaining that listeners and viewers would hunt for them. A surprising fact—not all of these commercials sold their products well. The talented writer, director and comedian, Mel Brooks, wrote and performed radio commercials for Ballantine Beer a few years ago. These were take-offs on a very successful record album he had produced previously. Listeners made it a point to hear these commercials again and again. Unfortunately for sales figures—these same listeners were not buying Ballantine Beer. But they loved the commercials!

## TELEVISION

Creating a television commercial is a form of *idea visualization*. There are those who think of television advertising as a print advertisement which has been animated. They also think of television commercials as radio with visualization. Both concepts are valid, up to a point. Television is much more—it is probably the most highly developed form of idea visualization which incorporates all of the elements of copy, art and layout previously discussed in newspaper, magazine, and radio advertising.

The relationship between copy and art in print advertising may be considered as the visual interpreting the verbal. In television, however, the relationship between art and copy should be the verbal interpreting the visual. If a viewer turns down the audio on a television commercial, the video should still have the ability to deliver the message.

The characteristics of effective advertising, discussed in Chapter 4, include the relationship of verbal and visual elements in advertisements and commercials, the need for a main appeal or unique selling proposition, and the value of simplicity to help send a clear message which will be understood, believed, and leave a strong impression.

The creation and production of television commercials demand a complex combination of skills. Writing, directing, set designing, casting, musical direction, art direction, filming, film animation, film editing and production are by no means a complete list, but should give you some idea of the need for expertise.

Very few retailers and only a few fashion producers and apparel manufacturers attempt to produce their own television commercials. Advertising agencies and television production specialists do practically all of the national network commercials, and most of the local retail productions. This preparation involves presentations which are part advertising layouts and part audio scripts.

These presentations which can describe television commercials of any length are called *storyboards.* (See Figure 52 for a typical agency-prepared storyboard of a fashion commercial.) The storyboard is a strip of video visuals (rough sketches or photographs) which are accompanied by the audio script and other information to *direct* camera procedure, use of actors and sets, voiceovers, sound effects, and music.

The storyboard like the print layout or radio script is a layout for a television commercial and a part of its planning and production procedure.

## OUTDOOR AND TRANSIT ADVERTISING

In billboards and transit advertising the visual must carry the burden of the message. Many print advertising campaigns repeat the same themes in outdoor and transit advertising with less copy. The time for reading a billboard is in most cases a fleeting instant. Transit advertising in a sense is a print ad mounted in a bus or train. The billboard must have the ability to send a message to an audience on the move at a distance. It has to be exceptionally clear and emphatic. Transit advertising enjoys a seated audience who may have nothing else to do but read messages, after they tire of studying people's faces.

In both these forms of advertising there is some competition by the distracting elements of being in transit or preoccupation with other reading or looking.

## DIRECT MAIL

The many possibilities for individual format and design in direct-mail media are limited only by the advertiser's ingenuity, budget, and what the post office will agree to mail for a price.

The copy and art elements are the same as for newspaper and magazine ads—the differences are a reflection of the use and format. Figure 53 illustrates most of the typical formats. Layout in direct mail advertising is a "dummy" or mock-up of the mailing piece.

*Figure 52. A storyboard of a television commercial prepared for a retailer for local television.*

*Figure 53. Various types of direct-mail media utilized by firms in the fashion industry.*

## DEALER AIDS

Dealer aids are any of a group of sales promotion material for advertising, display, publicity, fashion shows . . . which a producer will supply to a retailer to help him sell his customers. Following are examples of advertising dealer aids.

### DIRECT-MAIL TIE-INS

Statement enclosures, leaflets, catalogs or similar material that a manufacturer prints in quantity and supplies to a retailer for mailing to the retailer's list of customers. On this material a place is usually provided for imprinting the name and address of the dealer, so that the message seems to come from the dealer.

### RADIO AND TELEVISION TIE-INS

When a producer has an advertising campaign either by radio or television, this provides an excellent opportunity to tie-in with local retailers (dealers). If the manufacturer's line is carried by one or a few exclusive retailers in a territory, they may join in the program on a local participation basis, getting their own message in at the end of the commercial or wherever it will fit. Manufacturers often supply taped radio or television commercials with a blank at the end for the store's own message called a *tag* or *dealer "I.D."*

## OUTDOOR AND TRANSIT ADVERTISING TIE-INS

When a campaign of outdoor or transit advertising in a town is planned, the local retailer is told that if he will feature a branded line, his name will be printed on the outdoor advertisement or transit advertisement to inform customers where the merchandise can be obtained.

## THE NEWSPAPER AD MATRIX (MAT)

The *newspaper ad mat* is a device which enables a producer to provide a retailer with a finished newspaper advertisement featuring products which the retailer is buying for promotion. The ad mat is a treated composition material, similar to cardboard or plastic. It is actually an impression of the illustration and typography in an ad which has been photographically converted into "raised metal." This "raised metal" is the *photoengraving* and the *metal type* which was mentioned previously in our discussion of advertising production. The ad mat is a re-reproduction of the photoengraving and the type which can be produced in quantity at low cost, by rapid pressings of the metal photoengraving of the ad under great pressure. This works much the same as a wax impression of a key. The ad mat is lightweight and inexpensive. A 300-line ad mat can be produced in quantity for about 15¢ to 50¢ each, depending upon quality. It can be mailed to retailers who plan to advertise either on their own or on a cooperative advertising arrangement. The producer generally sends ad mats and proofs to retailers without charge. His cost per ad mat is often low enough so that he may include them in every merchandise shipment, whether it has been requested by the retailer or not. Figure 54 is a typical newspaper ad mat and proof which a fashion manufacturer has prepared for his retail dealers.

The retailer's local newspaper can duplicate the original photoengraving and type by casting a metal alloy into the ad mat. The mat

141

*Figure 54. A newspaper advertising mat and proof for a single item newspaper ad.*

material is capable of withstanding the high heat involved in this casting. This cast is called a *stereotype*. It can be cut apart in order to rearrange or eliminate elements of illustration and copy as directed by the advertiser.

The use of the newspaper ad mat is limited because it is prepared as a duplicate for many stores. It cannot be individual in its treatment of art, layout and copy. It is therefore rarely used by stores which have their own definitive style. The small retailer, who is not equipped or cannot afford to plan and produce effective newspaper ads, considers the ad mat an important dealer aid. Even in his case, he may often use parts of the ad mat, and by revising and substituting elements will make the finished advertisement more individual. The various stages involved in producing ad mats from original photoengravings and type, the casting of the stereotype from the mat, and the processing of the stereotype into the newspaper printing system result in a loss of fidelity in reproduction. This is another reason why newspaper ad mats have limited use. For hundreds of small retailers, however, the ad mat is an answer to getting better art and copy at a lower cost than they could possibly obtain themselves.

## COOPERATIVE ADVERTISING

### PROCEDURE AND PRACTICE

A manufacturer of a brand-name line of sportswear may say to the retailer, "If you will run an ad featuring my challis coordinates in your local newspaper, I will pay part of the cost." The share paid by the sportswear manufacturer may be fifty percent, or any other portion that is agreed upon. This is fundamentally the procedure used in *cooperative advertising*. It would seem that this arrangement should be ideal, and mutually advantageous to both the retailer and the manufacturer. Cooperative advertising, however, has its disadvantages along with its advantages. In order to understand these, let us examine a typical case . . .

A branded-apparel manufacturer makes an agreement with a retailer to pay fifty percent of the advertising space costs of any newspaper ads which the store will run. This agreement can specify the type of art and copy to be used in the ads and, in some cases, apparel manufacturers supply newspaper ad mats with art and copy, complete except for the price(s) and the retailer's name. The retailer runs the ad in his local newspaper. The newspaper bills the store for the space and the store pays it. The retailer then sends his own bill to the manufacturer, with a copy of the ad, showing what the manufacturer's share of the total newspaper cost is. The manufacturer then sends the retailer a check to cover that sum. This is a relatively simple and clear procedure. What are its disadvantages?

## DISADVANTAGES OF COOPERATIVE ADVERTISING TO MANUFACTURERS

1. Stores often do not give manufacturers the benefit of their lower retail contract rate, and they often charge a rate as high as the national advertising rate. The national rate is generally two to four times higher than the local rate.
2. Stores often run manufacturer's advertisements as part of departmentalized omnibus advertisements, and divide the total cost of space, including headings, copy and logotype, among various manufacturers. They also may charge for artwork and production when they create their own ads; rather than use the manufacturer's newspaper ad mat.
3. There is invariably a great amount of recordkeeping and accounting correspondence.
4. Despite warnings, stores are very slow in sending in bills and friction is the result.
5. Stores that have contracts with newspapers to use a certain amount of space a month, or a year, may use manufacturer's advertising on poor selling days, reserving good selling days for their own store promotions.
6. It is often difficult to control how a store will advertise the manufacturer's product. Many stores will not use a newspaper ad mat as supplied but will revise material that they feel emphasizes the manufacturer rather than the retailer. In making revisions, the store may eliminate elements which identify the manufacturer and complement his *national* advertising.
7. Much cooperative advertising is not coordinated with the store's planned promotions. There is a difference in style and content and little or no supplementation of window and interior display.

144

8. The competition between manufacturers may cause them to spend more money in cooperative advertising than is warranted.

9. Some retailers consider advertising allowances as discounts. Some will ask for a blanket "3 percent or 5 percent advertising allowance" for unspecified promotional efforts. The manufacturer can guard against this by paying only upon receipt of tear sheets of ads.

## DISADVANTAGES OF COOPERATIVE ADVERTISING TO RETAILERS

1. The lure to buy merchandise because of the influence of financial participation by the manufacturer in promotion.

2. Frequently the retailer is burdened with the launching of the promotion of comparatively little-known brands.

3. At the insistence of the manufacturer, cooperative advertising frequently lacks the ability to coordinate with the retailer's format. This practice also disrupts the identity and continuity of the retailer's advertising.

4. There is a possibility that the merchandise being cooperatively advertised is not in harmony with the store's philosophy and personality.

5. If the store buyer handles the cooperative advertising agreement, there is danger that the advertising director may not be consulted until it is too late to incorporate his thinking.

## ADVANTAGES OF COOPERATIVE ADVERTISING TO BOTH MANUFACTURERS AND RETAILERS

1. It gives the fashion manufacturer and the retailer additional exposure for their advertising dollar by sharing the advertising cost.

2. It can give a fashion brand the sponsorship of prominent retailers.

3. It may indicate to a manufacturer the degree of appeal of certain styles in his collection.

4. Retail advertising usually gets a better position in a newspaper than national advertising and is much lower in cost, because of the difference in rates between retail and national newspaper advertising space. This difference in rates is

being eliminated by many newspapers and by some local radio stations.

5. It can give a retailer identification with well-known and accepted fashion brands and their "name" designers.

## OTHER IMPLICATIONS

A section of the Federal Robinson-Patman Act requires that advertising allowances be made available to all stores on a proportionate basis *when the stores are located in the same marketing area.* A store is considered to be in the same marketing area when it competes for the same consumers' business. If there is doubt as to what constitutes a "marketing area," the U. S. Department of Labor's Bureau of Labor Statistics will provide answers to any questions regarding marketing areas. Still, there is always the danger of some store feeling that it has been discriminated against, even if not legally so. Cooperative advertising can create ill feeling by the retailer who feels he is not getting his fair share.

The pressure on fashion buyers from manufacturers offering to pay for cooperative advertising can get to be too high. The buyer should attempt to make the "best deal" only with those manufacturers whose merchandise is most wanted by his customers. If a buyer permits this allowance to sway his judgment and tries to promote anything but the most desirable fashion merchandise—he could be looking for trouble with his customers.

## CONCLUSION

Cooperative advertising can be of real value both to the store and to the fashion manufacturer. The terms should be clearly agreed upon in advance, including the schedule of space, dates, newspapers and the basis of charging. Total expenditures should be limited in some way, as in terms of a percentage of purchases. There should be agreement whether the advertisement is to be run by itself or a part of a departmentalized or "omnibus" store advertisement, and whether supplementary sales promotion is to be offered at the same time without further cost.

Written cooperative advertising agreements or contracts avoid many arguments as to what was actually in the arrangement. Most large companies have standard printed agreements ready for the dealer. They specify every possible detail right down to the correct size logo which the manufacturer requires for the advertising to be eligible for cooperative money. The written agreement serves also to prevent legal involvement with reference to preferential treatment of one dealer where others are to be granted the same or similar treatment.

Cooperative advertising can be an important part of the advertising plan. It should not be the reason for a buyer to feature or even stock an item, unless this merchandise is important to his customers.

# 8

# Publicity for Fashion News/Public Relations for Fashion Reputation

PUBLICITY IS DEFINED AS—An unsigned and *non-paid* commentary—verbal or written—in public information media. It is stimulated by interested parties seeking to present news about a company, its products, policies, personnel, activities or services. It can be a product or institutional promotion activity.

Any discussion of publicity invariably includes two other terms which are incorrectly used as synonyms for publicity, and vice versa. These terms are *public relations and advertising.* The reader should understand that public relations, publicity and advertising are related, but the differences between them are very fundamental. The following analysis indicates these differences and relationships.

PUBLICITY can result either from events that are deliberately *created,* or from an alert *coverage* of an event which will occur that is of interest to a firm's various "publics." The term "public" is used to designate various target audiences or groups. These are not always consumers. A company could consider that *competitors, vendors, employees, educators,* their *geographic community,* the *government* and their *customers,* each as a separate public.

Unlike advertising, publicity cannot be controlled. Where, when, and how the message appears cannot be directed by the publicity director. His only "control" is in suggesting and informing publication editors of the happening of news which would be of interest to the publication's readers. The publicity practitioner who uses a professional approach, and submits news which is of genuine value to a publication's readers, has the best chance to get his message in the *editorial matter* of a publication (or in the programming content of a radio or television station).

The practice of publicity does not rely on accidental happenings . . . it *plans happenings* and sees to it that the media are provided with the news.

Created or planned publicity is used or not used, subject to the judgment of the editor, columnist, or broadcaster who receives the material. Where and how it is used—in a column—in a feature story —or as a separate news story—is the decision of publication and broadcast editors.

For example, the same publicity material could be sent to several newspapers and magazines. It might well be treated in a very different way in each one. It could be developed as a feature story in a magazine, as a small news article in the fashion section of another, and be omitted from others. The distinction in any publication between *editorial matter* and *advertising* (or in radio or television, *programming* and *commercials*) is a most important one. Editorial matter consists of general news, feature pages, special sections, and columns which are written and supervised by news editors, fashion editors, business editors and the like.

Advertising is a paid message from any business or individual who cares to purchase the space. As long as an advertiser can pay for his ad, and comply with the *acceptability standards* of the publication, he can have his advertisement published. If a business or an individual knows of or develops an interesting "news angle" or news story about his firm, its products, policies or personnel—he can send it to editors for their consideration. Editors may include the story in the publication if they feel it is of genuine interest to their readers. An editor's job depends on sustained readership, viewing or listening which results in circulation or audience.

PUBLIC RELATIONS *is not sales promotion.* It is rather a long-range policy and program to create favorable public opinion about a firm. It is a sustained effort which serves as a guide for all communications with a firm's customers, vendors, employees or stockholders. As such, it helps set certain criteria for publicity, advertising, community relations, and the like.

A public relations *program* is concerned with everything that a firm does which will influence public thinking and attitudes. Publicity, advertising, and other sales promotion activities can be an important part of a public relations program.

Publicity is one way of communicating what a firm is doing in the *public interest.*

Advertising and promotion can also be contributors to a public relations program. In many firms where advertising is employed as the major contact with the customer public, it is in itself the prime component of the company's public relations program. Publicity, however, is considered by those who program its use as a better way of communicating for the purpose of good public relations. A firm's activities which may be in the public's interest is an excellent topic for news which is released for purposes of good public relations.

Advertising involves the sending of paid sales messages through various media. The space for these messages is purchased from various publications such as newspapers, magazines, outdoor and transit advertising; time is purchased from radio and television stations; postage is purchased for direct mail. Advertising is generally designed to produce sales. It is characterized mainly by the fact that it is *paid for* and *signed* (sponsored), and therefore directly controlled by the advertiser.

The advertiser selects the medium and decides when his message will appear. He writes the copy and determines the art and layout. What the advertisement says, and how it looks, is his responsibility and under his direction.

## WHY IS PUBLICITY SO IMPORTANT?

One of the most popular misconceptions in promotion practice is that publicity is "free advertising." This is a serious error since the ultimate use of publicity material is not under the *control* of the interested party. Advertising and publicity are basically different in that advertising is a message *from* the interested party, and publicity is a message from an information medium *about* an interested party. Publicity and public relations can work to create a belief in, and acceptance for a firm's advertising.

Publicity can be a unique form of product and institutional promotion because it involves the planning of a program to get influential editors, commentators, publications and personalities to say interesting and complimentary things about the firm, its personnel, and its activities. It is one thing for customers to read and hear from the firm itself just how good it is. It is also very impressive to customers to hear such things from more objective and authoritative sources.

## RESPONSIBILITY FOR FASHION PUBLICITY

The responsibility for fashion publicity is usually left to the professional practitioner. More and more producers of textiles and apparel are beginning to recognize the value of a publicity program in their sales promotion efforts. They are instituting new publicity departments or working with outside agencies and consultants. The large retailer is involved in a publicity effort which is handled by a special division or department. In many cases (which we will discuss later), the publicity program is combined with *special events*—especially on the retail level.

Although publicity programming and execution are the responsibility of the publicity department or agency, no firm could expect to do an effective job without additional help from within. This must come from those who know fashion and its customers most intimately. Buyers, salespeople, and fashion coordinators can contribute to the information and exposure which the publicist needs. For example, buyers help obtain photos from apparel manufacturers for their store publicity department. Buyers will also arrange editorial credits for their store in magazines which are featuring fashions which they have bought for their customers.

Fashion coordinators are very publicity-conscious. They will work with the publicity department to develop publicity for their own clinics and fashion shows—and also to stimulate publicity for fashion trends which they consider important for their customers. In some firms, the responsibility for fashion coordination and publicity is incorporated in one department.

## HOW DO YOU GET PUBLICITY?

An understanding of what is news and how editors evaluate news for their own publications is most important for the publicity person. The trite and obvious "You gotta know the right people" is indeed a misconception on how publicity is obtained. Knowing *who* are the right people to send publicity material to, and maintaining continuous and friendly contact with them, *is* important. It is essential to have a knowledge of the layout and content of newspapers and magazines which reach your audience. The same is true of the programming and schedules of broadcast—radio and television stations. An analysis of the average newspaper reveals that everything in it is not "news." The newspaper tries to give all of its readers good reasons to read its various sections and departments. Each print medium presents a varied menu of news, columns, editorial comment, special features, departments, feature pages, and supplement sections. Each broadcast medium has its own schedule of music, comedy, conversation, news, entertainment and public information. The publicity practitioner's responsibility is to write for some part of a newspaper's or magazine's editorial matter or for the programming portion of radio or television. The better acquainted he is with the requirements of the medium, the better he can develop his material for the medium's specific use.

## WHAT IS THE NATURE OF NEWS?

A large part of the publicist's job is to develop a happening or event so that it becomes genuine news or is at least possessed of intriguing or entertaining aspects that will make for interesting reading. A "news angle" may have to be invented through imaginative thinking. For instance, bridal collections are presented usually twice a year, but bridal gowns seldom show the kind of change which makes for news. What could be done to "make a fashion story" out of style trends in bridal gowns?

What type of fashion story is of genuine interest and value to readers of fashion pages and the new life-style sections? The following are general subjects which could serve as a guide for hundreds of different stories and features.

- *A new fashion trend* (The outdoor Western-inspired rugged boot instead of the fashion boot)
- *An improvement* (Natural fiber fabrics with new performance characteristics)
- *A synthesizing of related matters* (Sportswear and accessories appropriate for weekends in the country)
- *A response to current life styles* (Fashions for traveling, tennis, sailing, skiing, for private beaches or pools, skin and scuba diving, romancing)
- *A major business move* (Opening a new branch store, a newly decorated floor or a new department)
- *A "first" or an "exclusive"* (The discovery of a brilliant young designer by the store who decides for "adoption")

Knowing what is the nature of news, and being able to recognize and develop a news angle into a news story, is the first step towards obtaining publicity. The publicist must be an effective reporter, trained to dig for news. Understanding the needs of various publications will result in stories which can qualify as:

- *Straight News*—Important, exciting happenings and events.
- *Human Interest*—Stories of personalities, subjects which are meaningful to the life and welfare of the reader.
- *Feature*—The unusual angle, the surprise twist—not necessarily long, but heavy on appeal to the reader.

## THE PUBLICITY OUTLETS

The publicist must know *where* to send his story. A thorough knowledge of publicity outlets is valuable in a program to obtain publicity. The following is a partial list of examples.

### NEWSPAPERS

- Leading daily and Sunday editions
- Sunday supplements *(Parade, This Week, American Weekly, The New York Times Magazine)*
- Leading weeklies
- Trade newspapers *(Women's Wear Daily (WWD), Daily News Record)*

The types of stories for newspapers are:

- *General*—Prepared for main news sections, announcements, new policy, special events, changes in administration or procedure.
- *Departmental*—Slanted for a specific section or column (fashion pages, society, travel, food, entertainment, sports, business).

## MAGAZINES

- General national consumer weeklies (*The New York Times Magazine, Family Weekly* and other newspaper supplements)
- News weeklies *(Time, Newsweek)*
- Women's interest *(McCall's, Cosmopolitan, Good Housekeeping)*
- Home and Living *(Better Homes and Gardens)*
- Fashion Consumer *(Vogue, Glamour, Mademoiselle, Seventeen, Gentlemen's Quarterly)*
- Fashion Trade *(Men's Wear, Clothes, Earnshaw's Infants' and Children's Review, Sportswear Merchandiser)*

The special-interest story which is slanted to the selective audience of the magazine is more acceptable to magazine editors.

## RADIO

The rules for radio publicity are generally similar to newspaper publicity. The local interest or "hometown story" is especially effective. Here, the style can be more informal, and the particular delivery of the commentator who will receive your material should be kept in mind.

## TELEVISION

The most specialized and professional handling is required for television publicity. The skills of a specialist with considerable "TV know-how" is usually needed.

In the preparation of publicity material, the publicist must plan and write with the *type of story* or coverage firmly in mind. The *content* of his story—personal interview, fashion product news, fashion trends, institutional information—will help determine the type of story. The publicity material prepared will be designed for a newspaper column, special section, editorial, general section—or a magazine feature, department, photo layout—for a radio or television personality or commentary show.

## THE CONTACTS AND PLACEMENT

It is always important to have contact with "the right people." This does not mean that responsible editors can be influenced by bribes or cajolery to grant special publicity favors. An editor who abdicates his responsibility by putting personal interests ahead of those of his reader, listener or viewer does not last very long on a reputable medium The "puff-sheets" (jargon for publications which "sell" publicity along with advertising) are very obvious to the sophisticated reader.

It is important for the publicist to know who the editors and reporters are, when or where they can be reached, and the type of material they want and need. It is also important that editors and reporters know the publicist personally, and a friendly but professional relationship should be developed. A telephone should be used to give the press "tips" when appropriate. Whatever a publicist can do to help keep a publication informed will be returned in kind when a "break" on a story is requested. It is always good practice to include photographs with captions to accompany press releases, articles and features. It is frequently "guesstimated" that three-fourths of all editorial matter is suggested or "planted" by the interested party. The publicist's material, sent on a *consistent basis* to the *right person* at the *right time,* will be used when it is good, and when there is *room for it.* The professional publicist does not need to plead with or pressure editors and reporters. He should be helpful, patient, courteous and productive. He should keep good material coming, as much and as often as possible.

## THE PRESS RELEASE

The press release or publicity release is the most-used vehicle for transmitting publicity material from publicists to editors. Its format, style and contents vary, but certain elements are common to all. The press release illustrated here, is a good example of the most generally accepted format, and the reasons should be obvious to the reader (refer to Figure 55):

1. All copy is typewritten on 8½ × 11 white paper; no onion skin.

2. The format for the first page follows the style below:

Name of Company or Agency   Special to . . . (Exclusive)
Address: Street, City, State                For Release
Telephone                                            (DATE)
Name of writer

*HEADLINE IN CAPS, UNDERLINED*

Lead sentence starts about halfway down the page.

3. Double space copy, with at least one-inch, left and right margins.
4. Write on one side only; all pages numbered after first page; the word "more" is put at the end of each page until story ends.
5. Paragraphs should not be broken; end paragraph on same page. *Repeat key words of headline* at upper right of each page after first.
6. At end of story, put end mark ( # # # or —30—).
7. One story on a page only. Wherever possible, stories should be sent *Special to . . .* or *Exclusive.*

*Special to . . .*—Written specially for a publication.

*Exclusive*—No other paper gets this story in this area.

8. First-class mail should be used rather than mass mailings.

## CONTENT OF THE PRESS RELEASE

THE HEADLINE—The headline should present a capsule of the prime news interest of the story. It is not an attempt to write a headline for the publication. This is an editor's job. It should be comprehensive and emphatic. It should include an action verb.

THE SUBHEADLINE—This is optional and is used when it is necessary to supply an additional important fact.

THE LEAD—Usually a sentence or two which summarizes the news including the "5W's": *who, when, what, where* and *why.* Should an editor need to "edit" or cut a story even to the lead, the essence would still remain.

The next sentences or paragraph begins to fill in the story. Throughout the release, facts should be used in order of *diminishing importance.* This is sometimes referred to as an "inverted pyramid," which would have its base on top and narrowing down to the point.

156

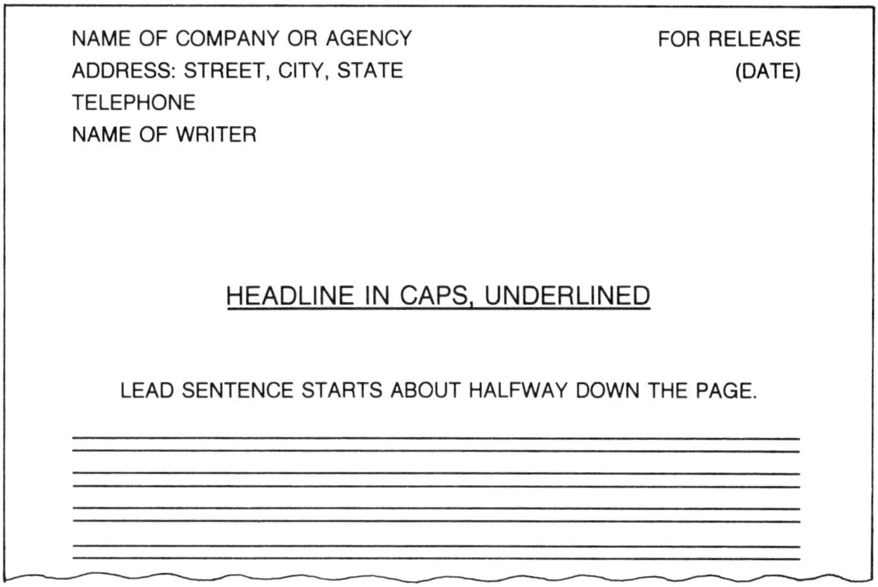

```
NAME OF COMPANY OR AGENCY                      FOR RELEASE
ADDRESS: STREET, CITY, STATE                     (DATE)
TELEPHONE
NAME OF WRITER




              HEADLINE IN CAPS, UNDERLINED


      LEAD SENTENCE STARTS ABOUT HALFWAY DOWN THE PAGE.
```

*Figure 55. The style and format of the press release.*

The important facts of a story should be on top and diminish down to a point of "diminished importance."

PHOTOGRAPHS—Fashion photographs are usually prepared with the format and visual style of particular publications in mind. Most of the fashion publications and special sections have staff photographers who have developed individual styles and techniques for their own editors. When photographs are included with press releases or other publicity material, the following general requirements should be observed:

1. Size, 8″ × 10″, or 5″ × 7″, glossy stock
2. Avoid "busy" backgrounds—emphasize people and fashions.
3. Captions should be typewritten in the same format as a press release and attached securely with rubber cement to the back of the bottom of photograph. (See Figure 57.)
4. Identify back of photograph in case attached identification is lost, being careful to avoid impression on photograph.
5. People should be identified from left to right. Full names, titles, firm affiliations are always included.

*Figure 56. A typical press release.*

FOR IMMEDIATE RELEASE                                    CONTACT: MARGOT INFANTINO

FALL FASHIONS AND ENTERTAINMENT STAR RAGGEDY ANN AND ANDY TEAM
FOR YOUNGSTERS AT GIMBELS  UPTOWN AND DOWNTOWN

A new fall sportswear collection of fashions for youngsters
sized 4 to 6x and Toddlers has arrived in Gimbels CHILDREN's WORLD at
Gimbels 33rd St. and Gimbels East at 86th street starring a special
leading lady and man -- Raggedy Ann and Andy.  The colorful beloved
cartoon and storybook characters based on original Rag doll designs show
up in charisma-charmed clothing in red/gold/navy-printed double-knit
polyester tops, blouses, pants, skirts and jumpsuits. Pictured is
a pint-size young fashionable on her way to see Gimbels special Puppet
show. produced by noted Puppeteer Rod Young featuring the delighful
Rag Dolls on SATURDAY, OCTOBER 9th. Youngsters will be admitted free
of charge but on a"first come come first served" basis at 11:30 a.m.

ONCE UPON A TIME-- the great Yves St. Laurent designed
a shirred bodice, tri-color jersey dress for little girls.
From the St. Laurent import collection exclusively for
Pumpkins & Monkeys-- the unique multi-level children's
shop at 801 Madison Avenue.


Price $135.

Sizes 4 to 14

Color: Royal/red/green tri-color


From Jerrie C.Rosenberg
     MILDRED CUSTIN LTD.
     502 Park Avenue  15 J
     New York, N.Y. 10022

     (212) 421-3974

*Figure 57. A typical fashion news photograph with caption attached as a press release. (Courtesy of Mildred Custin Ltd.)*

6. Written releases should be obtained from all models and people in photographs.
7. Credit all syndicated or stock news service photos; others as required.
8. Though a basic story may go to several publications, fashion photographs must be exclusive to each publication in any one area.

## STYLE OF THE PRESS RELEASE

Editors wants facts, not opinion, and can detect instantly a "build-up" or promotion for something really insignificant. The truth should be told. Honesty in publicity material will generate goodwill with editors. Clean-cut statements with full data, such as complete names and titles (sometimes with addresses in parentheses afterward) make for professional releases. It is better to include too many, rather than too few facts, as long as they are arranged in a quick-to-grasp and easy-to-edit format. An editor can cross out words, but should not have to spend precious time calling the writer for fill-in data. This applies especially in New York and other large cities, where newspapers almost invariably rewrite the story according to their own approach, so as to avoid duplication of what others are running. Copy in a release should be as near in style to the publication as possible. The publicist must determine what the publications want and give it to them.

Clarity of set-up for the release is most necessary to an editor whose desk each day is piled high with all kinds of communications. He must scan through these at top speed, and a format which enables him to grasp the story fast is a sign of professionalism, and is appreciated.

## THE TIMING OF PRESS RELEASES

Some stories are *advance announcements.* In this case verbs are in the future tense, e.g. "Macy's will open *The Cellar* on Monday, April 27 . . ." The publicist must beware of making assumptions which may prove false, such as, "a large, enthusiastic audience." A snow storm could keep an audience home, and one can only *hope* for an audience's enthusiasm.

Some stories can only be *reviews.* "Sales for the 52 week period ended December 31, 1977 were $50,000,000, the highest in the store's history."

Careful thought should precede a specific release dating. Any necessity for a *particular date of publication* makes news perishable. Who would plan a big Saturday fashion story for a Wednesday evening when papers usually devote so much coverage to foods? If the story fails to make the Wednesday page, it is dead. Saturday events are too late for Sunday, and dead for Monday. These should be written in future tense and released in advance for a *Friday* publication.

Some stories can be released for "Immediate" use, as an *exhibit of period furniture* which will last for several weeks, an *interview with a store personality,* or simple brief "fillers" about newsworthy but small individual items.

There is nothing as old as "yesterdays news." It is the responsibility of the publicity writer to consider the timeliness of his news and to give a release date which will allow the editor to present the story as close to the happening as possible.

## PUBLICITY RELEASES FOR BROADCAST MEDIA

These are prepared in basically the same way as press releases for print media. For radio, news is prepared in script form; and for television, in the form of slides, film strips or film clips.

# THE LANGUAGE OF PUBLICITY

Publicity writing should not be treated in a subjective manner. It should be written in the *third person; you, I* or *we* are never used! The writing should be handled as if the publicity writer were not an interested party, but rather an objective reporter. It is not *advertising copy,* which has a completely different purpose. It is not a literary composition, an essay, or a philosophical dissertation. These will rarely make the daily paper!

Editors want facts and reject such words as "marvelous," "fabulous" and superlatives which are *opinion* and overrate the facts. They also do not react favorably to last year's trite or hackneyed expressions, such as "Very here and now."

This does not mean that the writing has to be sterile. Fashion is more than a utilitarian covering. Fashion is more than seams and darts and textiles. Fashion is a "look," a mood, a coordination, taste, a living art. A vivid evocation of mood may, in its proper place, be considered factual reporting about fashion. This can be achieved through verbs and allusions, through solid writing rather than through an avalanche of adjectives. The active verb conveys far more spirit than passive forms. Some nouns hold a world of overtones. A look through any of the popular consumer fashion magazines will illustrate how richly expressive the language is. There are fashions in words used to describe color, style, silhouette. . . . The arts, history of costume, languages and theories of color all lend depth of perception and a new range of illusion to the writing of fashion.

## EDITORIAL CREDITS

When publicity materializes for a fashion manufacturer, it is the obligation of the editor to inform his readers of retail locations where the merchandise may be purchased. The naming of these stores in such publicity is an editorial credit (in this case sometimes called a "store credit"). Editorial credits may also include the names of designers, manufacturers, and often the suppliers of various accessories. It is of extreme importance that when a store credit appears, the merchandise should be available in the stores listed.

*Figure 58. This press kit for a unique multi-level children's shop describes in news format its unusual merchandise and services. (Courtesy of Mildred Custin Ltd.)*

## CONCLUSION

Publicity, like every other activity in promotion, must be planned, on a consistent basis. It must be properly executed by professionals who know how to "create" as well as "cover" the news. It should not be an activity which relies on the accidental incidence of news. The alert firm considers publicity as a *program* and will provide staff and budget for it. It is willing to evaluate its achievements over the long run and will institute this activity as an important factor in its product and institutional promotional program. A continuing effort, conditioned by realistic appraisal of *customer interest,* will usually give results which justify the time and expense.

# 9

## Display Is
## Visual Merchandising

DISPLAY IS DEFINED AS—A nonpersonal physical presentation of merchandise or ideas at the point-of-sale. It includes window, exterior, interior and remote display.

After all of the mass media activities of advertising and publicity have attempted to inform and motivate customers to come to the point-of-sale, it is the task of *visual merchandising* (window and interior display) to bring them to the point-of-purchase. Dramatic and compelling displays of merchandise in the windows and in the departments of a store are often more capable of persuading customers to identify with fashion themes and styles than advertising or publicity. It is the retailer's belief that display is a vital bridge between his mass communications and person-to-person selling. The term visual merchandising is a reflection of this point of view. It is becoming more common, even in "better" stores to see interior display and point-of-purchase display (P.O.P.) replace personal selling as forms of self-service.

### IMPORTANCE OF DISPLAY FOR EACH
### OF THE MARKET LEVELS

Producers and retailers both use display as a selling activity. Fashion producers and apparel manufacturers, however, are not so much concerned with display at their own point-of-sale as are re-tailers. Most of them do not have windows or anything else which might parallel the window display of a retailer. Many apparel manufacturers will present displays of their current line or collection in their showrooms—a form of interior display. In many cases these are retail-oriented to give window and interior display suggestions to store buyers. Manufacturers have also developed a large range of window and interior display aids which they supply to retailers in order to help sell their products. Some of these include: outdoor overhead signs, door signs, window props and materials, window banners and decals, interior overhead signs and banners, wall displays, shelf strips, counter cards, counter and wall racks and cases, floor racks, floor stands, and floor cases. We mention all of these because of the growing prominence of this important form of manufacturer-to-retailer aid which we previously referred to in our discussion of *dealer aids* (see page 140).

In our discussion of display in this chapter we will concentrate on the major uses of window and interior display by the fashion re-tailer.

## THE FOUR TYPES OF DISPLAY: WINDOW, INTERIOR, EXTERIOR, REMOTE

### WINDOW AND INTERIOR DISPLAY

No matter what kinds of merchandise a store handles or to what consumer group it caters, no matter what its type, size or financial strength, window display is among the store's most valuable methods for delivering a product or institutional message to potential customers. Many stores consider window display the most important of all forms of sales promotion. Often in fact, window display is the only form of promotion used, other than interior display. The high rentals paid by large department stores for sites affording good window display possibilities indicate the value that retailers attach to window display.

Window and interior displays are forms of sales promotion that are almost indispensable to every store. Window display helps a retailer to make sales inside the store by showing potential customers, through attractive window displays, the types and assortments of wanted merchandise carried in stock. Window displays, moreover, are at work while the store is closed, but interior displays work only while the store is open.* Both window and interior displays have advantages over other sales promotion activities in that they show the merchandise itself, rather than pictures or written descriptions of the goods. Numerous attention-getting devices such as color and mechanical motion can be utilized to present the merchandise most attractively. While other promotion activities reach prospective purchasers away from the point-of-sale, displays exhibit merchandise in the store itself. As a result, intentions to buy can be easily converted into actual purchases.

Window and interior displays have one very definite limitation which should not be overlooked. Because of their fixed position, displays are not seen unless people visit the store intentionally, pass the displays accidentally, or are attracted to the store by advertising or publicity designed to bring them there. Progressive retailers who wish to extend their trading areas and to increase their sales volume therefore recognize the necessity for supplementing displays with other forms of sales promotion (advertising, publicity, special events) which reach out for customers beyond the sidewalks surrounding their stores.

## EXTERIOR DISPLAY

Sometimes called *facade* display, this is largely for atmospheric and decorative purposes. Exterior display is most often ornamental and sometimes informational. It consists of material which is displayed on the *outside* of a store or business building.

Some examples are: Christmas trees, colored awnings, potted plants or special theme messages (Anniversary Sales). Examples of some uses of exterior display would be to "dress-up" a store for a special event, a seasonal promotion or a storewide theme.

## REMOTE DISPLAY

This is the only type of display which is "remote" or *away from the point-of-sale.* It is a display which a manufacturer or a retailer will set up in a hotel lobby, exhibit hall or airline terminal. It has the

*An exception is in the case of the "open window" display which will be discussed later in this chapter.

*Figure 59. A unique example of facade display in this Stix, Baer & Fuller, St. Louis, "built-out" window which converts them into walk-in, walk-thru old-fashioned shops.*

*Figure 60. Bloomingdale's, New York, sends an institutional message in this prestige window made up of 25 graphic posters featuring each of its holiday-inspired special shops.*

advantage of moving away from the point-of-sale to reach customers; the disadvantage of not being able to convert intentions to buy into immediate purchases.

## WINDOW DISPLAY

### IMPORTANCE OF WINDOW DISPLAY

Windows are the "looks," face and personality of a store. They provide the important first impression that a store can make on the customer. Windows function as an introduction of the retailer to the consumer. When they are used effectively they can contribute considerably to a store's traffic and sales volume. There have been many surveys to prove the effectiveness of window display. These have shown that the percentage of customers stopped by windows, out of all who are passing-by, compares favorably to the percentage of customers from the total circulation of an advertisement, who read and respond to the ad.

If you compare window display and advertising further, you can see several other common denominators. They have the same fundamental purposes, either (1) to sell merchandise immediately, or (2) to build a reputation over a longer period. In other words, as in advertising, there are "product and institutional" type windows. They must both fight for attention and interest yet register their impressions rapidly and emphatically. In the case of printed advertising we are dealing with two dimensions. In the case of window display we are operating in three dimensions. We could say, therefore, that some of the principles which make an advertisement effective also make a window display effective.

### ADVANTAGES OF WINDOW DISPLAY OVER ADVERTISING

Window display does have some obvious advantages over advertising as a sales promotion activity.

1. It is used at the point-of-sale.
2. Display presents the merchandise itself, life-size, in natural color, with fabric texture and other details easier for the customer to see.
3. Window shopping is a form of "entertainment"—it is a veritable "wishing world" for the customer who finds it easy to identify with the attractive mannequins.

Good display is capable of creating strong desire for merchandise even with the "just looking" customer.

## SHOULD WINDOW DISPLAY DUPLICATE ADVERTISING?*

Some stores regard window display as an activity separate from other forms of sales promotion. Their thinking, as mentioned before, is that window traffic represents a "circulation" similar to that of advertising and could be regarded as apart from other sales promotion media. On the other hand, there are stores who will try to duplicate the basic appearance of an advertisement, using display elements to convey the same theme and message.

## ADVANTAGES OF USING WINDOW DISPLAY AS A SEPARATE ACTIVITY

1. The selling productivity of each window can be more accurately evaluated.
2. Merchandise can be featured which is specifically suited to window display.
3. Windows can be kept more timely. For example, on rainy days the displays can feature umbrellas, rain boots and all-weather coats.

## ADVANTAGES OF USING WINDOW DISPLAY IN CONJUNCTION WITH ADVERTISEMENTS

1. The window could make it possible to reach customers who missed seeing the newspaper advertisement.
2. The repetition creates a strong impression on the customer that the store considers the merchandise and themes featured as especially worthwhile.
3. Buyers have an incentive to develop bigger and more original promotions when they are promised the double-action impact of an ad *and* a window.
4. Many merchandise managers and promotion directors believe that consistent and repetitive emphasis on important merchandise will produce greater sales. They believe that advertisements and window displays used in combination are much more productive than either might be alone.

*For the purposes of this comparison we are considering *print advertising* only. We are not including radio, television or other advertising media.

*Figure 61. Lord & Taylor, New York, does a selling window with more merchandise than they usually feature in their prestige windows. This one indicates their range of fashions for young customers.*

## TYPES OF WINDOW DISPLAY

Two general classifications of window display are *selling displays* and *prestige displays.*

*Selling displays,* like product advertisements, are designed to produce immediate sales by featuring the "right merchandise, at the right time, at the right price . . ."

*Prestige* or institutional displays are designed to impress customers with the leadership and originality of the store rather than to stimulate an immediate purchase. The purpose of prestige windows is to convince customers of the desirability of this store as a place to shop. Prestige displays make their appeal through the newness, the fashion-rightness, the exciting assortments, and the timeliness of the merchandise. It is apparent why the term "visual merchandising" has come into the language of retailing.

### SERIES DISPLAYS

*Series displays* are those in which several adjoining windows are used to display a common merchandise theme. A series display for a storewide Italian-import theme could feature: line-for-line copies of Italian designer dresses in one window, Italian leather gloves, belts and handbags in the second, Italian boutique accessories in the third, and so on.

*Figure 62. B. Altman and Co., New York, creates a series display effect with this elegantly divided window. The choice props (probably loaned from antique shops— who like the credit sign they get in the window) are a "series repeat" that helps set the mood of expensive luxury.*

*Figure 63. The Daniel Hechter Boutique in Paris does a related display window with active adventure à la the motorbike as a theme.*

## RELATED DISPLAYS

*Related displays* are those in which various classifications of related merchandise are placed in one window; thus they tell a complete merchandise story. For the apparel departments, a related display might be designed around fashion information which indicates that a certain green will be a popular color for fall sportswear and separates. Windows could thus feature various styles whose colors, patterns, and prints reflected different versions of this particular green.

SINGLE CATEGORY DISPLAYS—Some retailers have found that related windows, while attention-compelling, often lack the selling impact of windows which concentrate on only *one category of merchandise.* In the latter, all attention is directed to a single type of merchandise at one price. The main objection to related displays is that they show so many different items that none get the emphasis and attention which concentration could provide.

*Figure 64. Austin Reed Ltd., London, presents the "Safari" look for men in this dramatic single category window display. Appropriate accessories are featured—but the merchandise category is primarily the safari suit.*

*Figure 65. This Bonwit Teller, New York, window is an excellent example of the use of the open window—the network of roping is creative window design, which also permits a clear view of the men's store within.*

## CAMPAIGN WINDOW DISPLAYS

*Campaign window displays* are those in which the same type of merchandise is featured week after week in the same windows. The windows may change, but the merchandise category and fashion theme keep repeating a specific sales message. For example, campaign displays can be effective in establishing a reputation for a particular designer, style trend, brand or price line through repetition. The success of campaign displays demands that they appear in the same windows each week, and the display design employed should have recognizable continuity.

## SINGLE-PROMOTION DISPLAYS

*Single-promotion displays* are those in which one major selling event is featured in all or most of the store's windows. Most stores have traditional annual promotions which are important enough to assign all or most of its windows. Under the single-promotion display plan, all windows might be devoted to annual "home redecorating weeks" with displays of many different rooms of furniture and home furnishings.

With all this emphasis about the value and impact of window display, it is understandable that some readers may well wonder if window display is increasing at the expense of other activities of sales promotion. The answer is "no."

Some stores are being built today with solid walls adjoining entrances, and no windows. It is important, however, to note that such architecture is usually confined to shopping centers where customers drive to a parking lot and head straight for the store doors. There are no so-called pedestrians to stroll along and to window-shop.

Such store planning is not confined only to shopping centers and shopping malls. Increased costs of display staffs and display materials have resulted in smaller and fewer windows in recent new store and branch store openings. Some of these windowless stores have built small shadowbox-type windows for most-wanted items. Those solid walls in these new buildings serve a purpose, too. They are often used for next-to-department stock space, just behind selling areas.

Another trend is the construction of the open window which provides the passer-by an open view of all the "goodies" inside. The growth of shopping centers and shopping malls offers store architects many varieties of store layouts. Traffic patterns and location call for individual planning. More on the open versus the close window later in this chapter.

## HOW DO RETAILERS ASSIGN WINDOWS?

There are two distinct policies which retailers use in assigning windows. One is the *departmental method* which assigns certain windows to certain departments for regular displays. The second is the *rotation method* which rotates windows from one department to another, attempting to expose the widest assortment of merchandise to customers. The method which is used depends upon the specific merchandising policy of the store. It is important that the windows reflect the store's attitudes towards fashion trends, fashion themes, brands and styles. If a store's policy is to emphasize its concentration on certain brand names and price lines of apparel, then its major windows should feature these categories. Other merchandise would be assigned to windows which are not as prominently located.

If the store is trying to launch one of their own private-label brands, this merchandise should be featured in the windows. When a store is known for doing an outstanding job in a certain department, this would encourage a policy which would constantly show that merchandise in the major windows. The assigning of windows is therefore a responsibility of those in the store who determine the store's fundamental merchandising objectives and service role to the consumer.

In specific situations the assigning of windows should also consider the following criteria:

1. The selling effectiveness of similar displays previously used.
2. Seasonal appeal and timeliness of merchandise.
3. Which categories of merchandise in which departments are being emphasized in the store's sales promotion plan.
4. The supplementary sales promotion activities which will be used.
5. The specific suitability for window display of this merchandise.
6. Suitability of the merchandise for combination with merchandise from other departments in related displays.
7. The prestige which the store could receive from this particular display.

## HOW ARE WINDOW DISPLAY COSTS DETERMINED?

Store windows are among the most valued areas of space in the store. The importance of window display as a sales promoter and traffic builder is universally accepted. Windows that face busy thoroughfares are especially prized. Their share of rent charged is usually higher per square foot than other areas in the store.

The general practice among retailers is to prorate the costs of display. These costs include: the specific rent or lease or amortization charge for the window space, together with its proportional share of the costs of display props, fixtures and materials; the salaries of the display director and his staff; and the other variable costs such as lighting and maintenance. The "costs" of window display are charged to each selling department on a previously established proportionate basis. The criteria for "giving a buyer a window" is seldom based upon anticipated volume, since the windows are not as flexible a supply of sales promotion as advertising. For example, you can buy an extra page of newspaper advertising. . . .

## HOW OFTEN SHOULD WINDOWS BE CHANGED?

Surveys of retail stores in large cities have revealed that most stores change their window displays once a week. Stores in smaller cities will tend to change windows more often. This is because the store in a small city or town, located in a compact business district, is likely to have its customers pass its windows more than once a week. On the other hand, the metropolitan store located in a large, spread-out business area may not have people passing its windows even once a week. The exception would be those customers who are employed in the vicinity of the store.

Regardless of location, however, each store must determine its own policy on frequency of change. The following questions related to the problems of the specific store could be asked:

1. What is the nature of the neighborhood location?—Is it business or residential? A store in a residential section would have its windows seen more often by any one customer than a store in a business district.
2. What type of merchandise does the store carry?—What is its "personality" and the nature of its service to customers? For example, is it necessary for a wallpaper and paint store to change its window displays as often as an apparel boutique?
3. How many people will pass the windows each day? A store located in a high traffic area might have to change its window displays more often.

### WHAT ARE THE ADVANTAGES OF FREQUENT CHANGE?

1. Displays can be more timely—and can tie-in with the most current fashion trends.
2. Customers are exposed to a greater variety of merchandise.
3. Merchandise is less likely to be damaged by soil and fading from the sun. Merchandise left in windows too long can result in expensive markdowns, if the merchandise gets soiled or faded.

*Figure 66. The closed window has dramatic possibilities which open windows cannot offer. This Saks Fifth Avenue, New York, window draws the passer-by into a very realistic bistro full of atmosphere conducive to the fashions being featured.*

## OPEN AND CLOSED WINDOWS

A recent innovation in the design of new stores has been the use of *open* windows instead of *closed* windows. The open window eliminates the conventional closed-in compartment which we see in so many stores. The open or "see-through" windows permit customers passing by to get an unobstructed view of the interior of the store. The open window has been most popular with stores in shopping centers which depend largely on automobile traffic rather than passer-by traffic. The boosters of open windows maintain that customers of shopping centers (except those centers with networks of promenades) arrive with specific purchases in mind, leave their cars in near-by parking lots, and then go quickly to previously selected stores. There is no necessity or time for window shopping. Under these circumstances open windows are all that are needed.

The open window has the following advantages:

1. It moves selling areas closer to the customer on the sidewalk.
2. An immediate impression of the interior of the store is conveyed to the busy passers-by.
3. Customers can see the activity inside and may be impelled to "join in."
4. The initial construction cost and subsequent maintenance of open windows is less than closed windows.

There may be much to say for the open window in shopping centers that do not have public sidewalks. But many retailers still object to the "see-through" window. They feel that the open window has the following disadvantages:

1. It is very difficult to emphasize a single item or an idea.
2. The open window does not permit as dramatic a merchandise or institutional display as the closed window.
3. It creates a "fishbowl" atmosphere in which customers and the interior of the store are "on view."
4. It reveals the interior of the store when it is empty, and may discourage customers from entering.
5. It gives up the stock space offered by the interior walls of closed windows.

The question of closed versus open windows necessitates the study of the advantages and disadvantages of each type. The type of store and its particular location are the main determinants. If a retailer expects a large volume of passer-by traffic, the closed window probably offers more possibilities for dramatic selling windows.

## THE ELEMENTS OF WINDOW DISPLAY

In the two-dimensional advertisement we are dealing with elements of art and copy which we arrange or "layout" into the space available. In window display we are using physical rather than graphic elements, arranging them in space for maximum attention and selling effect. These physical elements are:

1. The *Merchandise* itself, apparel and/or accessories.
2. *Functional props* which include mannequins and body forms which "wear" apparel or abstract props or fixtures which hold merchandise.
3. *Decorative props* are used to establish a mood or setting for merchandise.

178

*Figure 67. Lord & Taylor, New York, often uses the merchandise itself to serve as props and background as in this sophisticated window featuring furnishings with animal motifs.*

4. *Structural props* which support functional and decorative props, fixtures, mannequins or other units. Structural props are architectural in design and can change the organization and physical contours of the window.
5. *Backgrounds.* The back and side walls of the window (discussed in detail later in this section).
6. A great variety of *Display materials* . . . as wide a selection as creative imagination (and budget) will allow. These are used for floors, walls, decoration, pictorial setting and atmosphere.

In practice, the effective use of these elements is based upon the same criteria which apply in other sales promotion activities. The customer must be attracted, his interest aroused by merchandise (or ideas about it), and he must be given specific reasons to buy suggested by *his* wants and needs. The display director must use his creative skills to make display dramatic and attractive. His first

179

*Figure 68. La Rinascente, Milan, uses a structural prop, a double-row platform, and a mannequin to display its White Sale.*

responsibility, however, is to fulfill the buyer's and the store's sales objectives.

## COLOR

Colors suggest many different things to people. There are certain responses to color which are generally assumed to be universal. For example, red suggests heat and fire . . . excitement. Yellow suggests gaiety and the sun. Green is cool and relaxing. Blue is soothing, like the sea and sky. White is usually associated with purity and cleanliness. Black and gray are neutral and are therefore well suited for walls and backgrounds. Other colors seem to blend into these neutrals.

## LIGHTING

Natural daylight is largely composed of cool blue light, while artificial light is largely warm and yellow. In practice, display directors use yellow light for merchandise which is worn at night. Merchandise for daytime use can be shown under daylight blue lighting. Warm lighting acts to neutralize cool colors and intensifies warm colors. Cool light neutralizes warm colors and intensifies cool colors.

## BACKGROUNDS

The purpose of the background in window displays is to provide the merchandise with a framework that will create an appealing mood or realistic setting which will demonstrate the use of the merchandise.

The two basic types of background are: (1) the *decorative* background and (2) the *pictorial* background. The decorative classification includes all *fixed* backgrounds, such as wood panels and draperies. It also includes *movable* backgrounds, screens and panels. Decorative backgrounds are designed to serve as an ornamental framework for the merchandise. The pictorial backgrounds provide the merchandise with a realistic environment similar to theatrical scenery. It suggests when, where, and how merchandise can be enjoyed. This is why many display directors prefer it to the less dynamic decorative background.

## WHEN SHOULD SIGNS AND PRICES BE USED?

DESCRIPTIVE SIGNS—Most stores believe that descriptive signs are an essential element to all window displays. Many stores have a policy that no merchandise can be displayed without descriptive signs. Signs can mean as much to a window as copy to an advertisement. A sign can present a merchandise theme, introduce a fashion trend, feature a designer, give the background of a product, tell why it is desirable, why it is an excellent value, and so on. Window signs can be printed or handlettered. They must follow the "look" of the entire display, much the same as typography style in an ad. The sign should be legible and easy to read. The copy should be concise and not attempt to go beyond one important keynote. Too many appeals can confuse the onlooker so that no message gets through. Generally, the principles for advertising copy would also apply in the writing of window signs.

PRICES—Except for certain exclusive shops, most stores follow a policy of pricing merchandise in their selling windows. These stores

*Figure 69. Not every store will use price tickets such as in this Austin Reed Ltd., London, men's wear window. But it's a rare window which would omit a sign which so effectively presents its items of "Art Deco at Cue."*

may have just as many prestige windows without prices. Many stores control the emphasis that they place on price, by varying the lettering, shape, size and color of price cards and tickets.

## HOW IS BALANCE USED IN WINDOW DISPLAY?

As in an advertising layout, balance is an essential quality of a well-designed display. It involves the arranging of merchandise and props around the center in such a way that their weights will bal-

182

ance when they are equally distributed. Symmetrical balance is obtained by placing two objects of the same weight at equal distances from the center. Informal balance is obtained by placing heavier units toward the center and lighter ones away from the center. Formal balance arranges a large unit in the window's center of interest with the lighter units in harmony with it to provide symmetry.

FORMAL BALANCE—Used when it is desirable to have a dominant point of interest in the display with subordinate elements each having equal attention-power.

INFORMAL BALANCE—Used when the units to be displayed vary their attention-power but are arranged in a dynamic balance. The difference in attention-power may be caused by shape, color or arrangement. Informal balance lends itself to dissimilar units.

To achieve attractive balance in window display, one should also consider *proportion.* By proportion we mean:
1. The shape or size of one display unit as related to another;
2. The shape or size of the unit as related to the window itself.
Windows are most interesting to the eye when space relationships and proportions are varied.

When units of different heights are used in window display, the general practice is to arrange larger units towards the rear of the window with smaller units or those which have intricate detail toward the front.

## A CHECKLIST FOR EFFECTIVE WINDOW DISPLAY

Some guidelines to follow suggested by the experience of many display directors:
1. *Planning.* Good window display is a product of careful planning and scheduling. The components of an effective window need to be planned in advance with enough time for preparation and installation.
2. *The merchandise should be in demand.* Windows, just as much as advertisements, should feature merchandise in which customers have indicated high interest. What will be

fast-selling is usually effective in windows. Merchandise with high impulse to buy will make the windows more productive, and customers will be impressed that the store has the right merchandise at the right time.

3. *Timeliness.* Window displays should be in tune with whatever is current. The display director should be alert to all that is happening in his area, in order to capitalize on events of public interest. For example, the opening of the opera season could suggest a theme for evening wear and accessories.

4. *The policy and character of the store should determine how much merchandise.* The right amount of merchandise for a window display is very important. There are no concrete rules concerning the number of items that should be featured. This depends upon the character of the store and what it wants to say to its customers. The important thing is that the merchandise should demonstrate, in assortment and quality, the basic appeal of the store itself.

5. *Merchandise should be suitable for window display.* A window display should not include merchandise which is out of proportion to its setting. Large pieces of furniture, for example, should be placed in a window large enough to enable customers to visualize how it might look in a room. Smaller items, such as fashion accessories, should be displayed in smaller settings, to prevent merchandise from looking lost in a disproportionate large space. Generally, bigger items should be placed further back from the glass and small items should be brought close to the glass so that important details can be examined by customers at comfortable eye-range.

6. *Simplicity.* Simplicity is a good general rule for all categories of design. Window display is no exception. An overworked, overcluttered display works against its sales objective because it is not readily understood. The customer does not receive a single, emphatic impression.

7. *Lighting.* Lighting can be a key to effective or ineffective window display. Customers must be able to see merchandise clearly in order for it to arouse their interest and desire to buy. Inaccurately directed lighting creates glare and makes it difficult to see any of the units clearly. Improper distribution

of light obscures certain units of display and creates unattractive shadows and too much reflection. If the display designer wishes to emphasize certain units and de-emphasize others, he can direct his lighting accordingly.

8. *Cleanliness and Order.* It goes without saying that the window must be neat and clean. It is surprising how many stores fail in this respect. Cleanliness in display involves more than the merchandise. Mannequins, props, fixtures, walls, flooring, glass and signs must be clean and in good order. Customers are repelled by cracked noses, crooked wigs and dead insects. Windows should be checked regularly (each day) to spot any imperfections in cleanliness and order.

## INTERIOR DISPLAY

More and more stores now consider interior display to be one of their most important sales promotion activities. They regard interior display as a necessary partner of window display and advertising. Effective interior display can supplement those sales promotion activities which contact customers before they come to the point-of-sale. Interior display can act as a kind of insurance for the effort and expense of advertising and window display activities.

### WHY DO STORES PLAN INTERIOR DISPLAY?

1. *Location*—Interior displays help customers to locate merchandise which they have seen in windows and ads.
2. Interior displays *help salespeople to sell* merchandise by providing additional information and selling points to customers.
3. Interior display can *suggest a related item* to a customer and help salespeople to build a larger sale.
4. Interior displays give each department an opportunity to *bring* its *merchandise out where customers can see it,* sometimes providing the only sales promotion activity other than personal selling.
5. Interior displays can provide the store with a new *personality* for seasonal and storewide events. This can be done throughout the store or in separate departments.

*Figure 70. Interior display has a great variety of artistic expression—which also helps create a stimulating environment which adds to the excitement of fashion. It also sells.*

*There is no doubt about the season or the merchandise in this interior "gateway" to a Bloomingdales, New York, outerwear department.*

*Air space used for a life-size shadow box effect by Rich's of Atlanta.*

186

*Bergdorf Goodman, New York, uses floor and aisle space to display merchandise in its "Covent Garden Dance Shop."*

*What's the middle of a floor for? An island display in Saks Fifth Avenue, Hackansack, N.J., adds a dramatic emphasis to a department.*

187

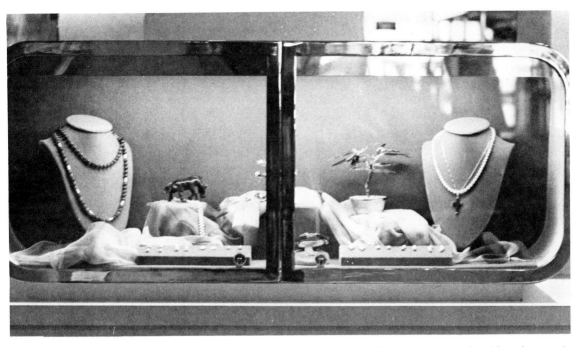

*Figure 71. "Case studies" in display. These stylized cases not only add to the store's interior decor—they also suggest related merchandise. (Left: Pumpkins & Monkeys, New York. Right: Thalhimers, Richmond, Virginia.)*

## TYPES OF INTERIOR DISPLAY

Most retailers find that their interior display problems are as individual as the character and physical facilities of their store. Each will develop his own methods and techniques.

Most interior display, however, can be classified as follows:
1. Showcase displays
2. Counter displays
3. Environment displays
4. Wall, ledge, aisle and island displays

The buyer or department head can work with the display director to determine which kind of interior display will be most effective for his merchandise and department. He must analyze the department's space and traffic patterns and decide what are the sales objectives of his interior display. Interior display should be developed

189

from the character of the merchandise itself as well as the look which the department head wants for the department.

## SHOWCASE DISPLAYS

There are several kinds of showcase displays, all characterized by their *degree of accessibility to the customer.*
1. Sides of selling cases where merchandise can be seen through the glass.
2. The glassed-in wall cases behind the counter where stock is kept but where merchandise is also visible.
3. Shadow boxes: Open, recessed areas above and behind the selling counter.
4. Interior windows: Usually built into spaces alongside doorways, elevator banks, escalators and staircases.

## COUNTER DISPLAYS

A display on a selling counter must be limited because of the danger that it might interfere with personal selling and obscure other merchandise which customers should see. There are other items beneath glass counters in cases which counter displays should not hide. Counter displays are important and can be effective in helping salespeople to illustrate and convince customers of selling points necessary to create the desire to buy.

## ENVIRONMENT DISPLAYS

Environment displays are basically different from the typical selling displays. Of course, the purpose of both is to sell, but the approach is different. In the environment display, merchandise is placed in a realistic, life-size setting which helps customers to walk into it and imagine the satisfactions which they could obtain from owning it. Furniture, appliances, rooms, and even parts of houses are featured in environment displays.

## MISCELLANEOUS DISPLAYS

There are several other miscellaneous interior display techniques which stores use, as their space and facilities allow.

WALL AND LEDGE SPACES can be utilized as display areas. Substantial amounts of unused wall and ledge spaces can be developed into effective and attractive store and departmental displays.

*Figure 72. Marshall Field, Chicago, makes ingenious use of structural props, decorative props, mannequins, fixtures and various adapted display materials to provide interior displays throughout its store.*

ISLAND DISPLAYS, like wall displays, can use to advantage areas of floor space which might otherwise be idle. Every store can find certain areas where traffic is light enough to permit free standing display units. When these are placed at the end of an aisle which comes to a deadend, they are called *aisle displays*.

## HOW DOES INTERIOR DISPLAY SELL?

Any of the forms of interior display could be further classified by sales objectives:
1. To present assortments
2. To introduce ideas
3. To suggest related merchandise

- *Presenting Assortments*—An assortment display shows the customer a wide range of merchandise, which can include styles, colors, fabrics and prices.
- *Introducing Ideas*—Displays which present background information, new uses and care of merchandise, or the "romance" of the particular item or its designer.
- *Suggesting Related Merchandise*—Related merchandise is grouped to promote an associate sale and help the customer visualize how certain items of merchandise will look and act with others.

## WHO USES INTERIOR SIGNS AND PRICES?

The character of the store will largely determine whether interior signs and price cards should be used. Our previous discussion on signs for window display generally applies to interior display. Except for a few exclusive specialty stores, most stores use interior signs and prices.

The variety of signs used by stores include the following:
1. Counter Signs
2. Hanging Signs
3. Banners and Flags
4. Elevator Cards
5. Posters
6. Easels

## WHO IS RESPONSIBLE FOR WINDOW AND INTERIOR DISPLAYS?

The display responsibility in a retail store is divided between the merchandising and display divisions. Department heads are responsible for the selection of merchandise and themes which will satisfy the objectives of the store's Sales Promotion Plan. They must develop ideas which will sell merchandise *and* the store to the customer.

The display director and his staff are responsible for the translation of sales objectives into effective and attractive display design. The display must sell merchandise and the store. It must contribute to the prestige and personality of the store.

The display division is responsible for all window equipment, materials, signing and maintenance. The display staff designs, and executes window displays. They effect the unity and coordination of window display and storewide interior display. This includes walls, columns, ledges, doorways, elevators and other "free areas" which are designed for storewide display.

In many stores, buyers and department heads handle their own interior display, calling upon the display department for fixtures and signs. In this case a request is filed for whatever equipment and material is required, with the copy for the signs written by the buyer and his assistants. Departmental interior display, since it is concerned mainly with the arrangement and selling of merchandise, is often executed by experienced salespeople in the department, who have been assigned this responsibility by the buyer.

Often buyers will request *special departmental displays* which the display department can plan and execute. This is similar to the procedure used for requesting an advertisement or a window display. In cases where merchandise is loaned to the display division for other than departmental display, *loan slips* are used as a receipt for such merchandise. Thus merchandise which is outstanding for more than a prescribed period of time can be recorded and recalled.

## CONCLUSION

Many retailers consider window and interior display to be of equal importance. The display departments of some large stores maintain separate interior display directors and display staffs and will assign a staff member to each floor or to certain departments. No matter what its size, no store can afford to be without display. The exceptions are the new "windowless" buildings which are constructed for stores which make up for it with highly creative interior displays. There are also volume/low-price stores which attempt to presell their merchandise with extra-heavy advertising and publicity budgets. Such stores do less in interior display and their "selling from pipe racks" is incorporated as part of their image to customers. The general trend, however, is in the direction of innovative and better display, if not more display.

Some manufacturers who recognize the assets of dramatic visual merchandising are using street-level showrooms and remote display to sell their products and ideas to buyers. They use their selling showrooms to feature interior display at the point-of-sale. The excitement of fashion apparel involves all of the senses—with sight and touch high on the list. Effective display allows one to see and feel and react to this excitement.

# 10

# Fashion Shows
# Are Live Promotions

Of all the activities in the promotion of fashion, the fashion show stands out as the most dramatic and compelling. When it comes to presenting the excitement and drama of fashion, no other form of promotion can compete with a fashion show. The reason for this is implied in the name and definition of a fashion show itself. It is a show. In every sense of the word. Every element of theater is incorporated together with its devices and its procedures. The fashion show can be simply defined as: "Presentations of merchandise in living and moving form."

The fashion show, like all other promotion activities can take many different forms. It also "plays to different audiences." It has different sponsors and different uses.

## WHY IS THE FASHION SHOW IMPORTANT
## TO THE FASHION INDUSTRY?

One of the most popular current theories in effective selling is the one which counsels—"If you want to sell—influence the influentials." There is something about the fashion show with its advance notices, first opening, and theatrical production, which makes its audience feel influential. The effective show can generate in its audience a feeling of being let-in on the newest and most important developments in the world of fashion. The very successful shows have an "in-crowd" audience of cognoscente fighting for admission, creating a syndrome of excitement which carries through the coming season. This occurs on all market levels: The haute couture of the Chambre Syndicale in Paris with its audience of professional buyers and world press; the Deering-Milliken highly staged and professionally cast trade shows for designers and apparel producers; the consumer shows of prominent retailers. Despite the limitations in audience size (as compared to other activities using public information media) the fashion show's power to influence those who influence others—the designers, the buyers, the retailers, the press and the in-customers—make it a most important product and institutional promotion activity.

Among the important reasons for staging a fashion show are prestige, the introduction of new lines and designs, and the building of goodwill. Frequently a fashion show is given to impress a public of the store's fashion alertness and leadership.

## TYPES OF FASHION SHOWS

There is some variance of terminology in this area. Many sponsors of shows will call their productions fashion shows which others would consider as merely "showings" or informal shows. For the purpose of clarity we will classify fashion shows as *formal* or *informal.*

*The Formal Show* is a show with an identifiable theme; a staged production; a script and commentary. It generally has an invited audience which is usually seated. It incorporates all or most of the elements of theater.

*The Informal Show or "Showing"* is a presentation whose theme is not as emphatically identified as in the formal show. It relies on a comparatively loose structure with production, staging and direction not as tightly planned and rehearsed as in the formal show. The informal show does not always have a script and commentator—the audience reads descriptive information from cards or programs.

The difference in the two types of shows is mainly a matter of degree. They both rely on some theme, some sort of descriptive commentary, some production and staging. When the production is "all-out theatre" we consider it a formal show. When a more informal structure is used, we consider it an informal show or showing. In many cases, *strict* classification could be a problem. The showing is more likely to be considered as personal selling than nonpersonal promotion.

## TYPES OF FASHION SHOWS CLASSIFIED BY AUDIENCE AND SPONSOR

Both formal and informal fashion shows are used by each of the market levels in the fashion industry. Each is playing to its own audience; each has its own sales objectives. Fashion shows can also be classified by sponsor and audience.

### THE INDUSTRIAL OR TRADE SHOW

The industrial or trade show is sponsored by a producer of raw materials (usually textiles) or a manufacturer of apparel. The audience is usually composed of professionals and/or the press. In the case of the raw materials producer, the audience will include apparel designers, piece goods buyers for apparel producers, retailers, and the press. The objectives of such shows are to demonstrate the versatility, utilization and appropriateness of the material product in the designing and manufacturing of fashion. The apparel designer and manufacturer will play to an audience of retailers and the press with the objective of selling their interpretation of fashion trends and tastes. The fashion creators seek to differentiate their collections in terms of originality and value appeal to the consumer.

Several of the prominent consumer fashion magazines also sponsor shows which, in effect, could be called trade shows. Sometimes referred to as *fashion clinics,* these shows present fashions from many apparel producers which represent the magazine's editorial viewpoint on what is important and exciting, and which they hope will be featured by their editors. It is no mere coincidence that these shows also promote the sale of advertising pages by featuring merchandise which their advertisers have already inserted in the coming issues. The audience will frequently include many levels of the fashion industry: raw materials producers and apparel manufacturers and retailers, and members of the press.

197

## THE RETAIL SHOW

The retail show is sponsored by the retailer for presentation to many different types of audiences. Each of these has a different objective which might have very little effect on its structure.

THE *INTERNAL* OR *IN-STORE SHOW*—Designed to inform store personnel of the what's new and exciting which the store will promote. Its purpose is to acquaint its audience with the merchandise, stimulate their enthusiasm, suggest selling points, and sales approaches. It serves to implement sales promotion planning throughout all levels of the store.

THE *CUSTOMER SHOW*—A presentation to customers which features storewide, seasonal, departmental, designer, private label, or manufacturer-brand themes. It is designed to sell merchandise, and ideas which sell merchandise. Manufacturers will cooperate or provide the elements for a consumer show which features their brand exclusively, or presents their style collection with some prominence. They will send special sales representatives to present "trunk showings" of merchandise to customers in the store, in advance of the selling season. These are very informal and are usually presented right on the selling floor. (These, too, could be called a type of personal selling.)

THE *COMMUNITY* OR *CHARITY SHOW*—Co-sponsored by the store with a local institution or fund-raising charity. The objectives, in addition to selling the merchandise, are institutional—increasing goodwill, and building a strong community position.

## THE PRESS SHOW

The press show is a special performance for members of the press usually given in advance of the "regular performance." This is a practice of the larger trade and retail sponsors who wish to ensure themselves of substantial press publicity.

# FASHION SHOW PLANNING

Probably the most important factor in a successful fashion show is the process of thoroughness in planning. No detail may be left to chance and no phase of the show should be presented without rehearsal.

## THE BUDGET AS A CHECKLIST

In planning a fashion show, the end consideration, of course, includes audience, size of audience, and purpose of the show. An experienced producer of fashion shows would quickly admit that the character and scope of the show depends heavily upon the budget. Depending upon its specific purpose and theme, every fashion show does not have all of the following items to be considered in a budget, but it is well to use some type of checklist to be certain that there is budget to cover the following:

1. Rent (if any)
2. Porters
3. Transportation
4. Stage and Runway Construction
5. Curtains
6. Electricians
7. Props
8. Advertising and Publicity
9. Lights
10. Public Address System
11. Alterations
12. Pressing
13. Tickets
14. Posters
15. Programs
16. Model Fees
17. Commentator Fee
18. Overtime
19. Meals
20. Music
21. Depreciation of Merchandise
22. Insurance

# HOW DO YOU PRODUCE A GOOD SHOW?

The following is an adaptation from "Let's Have A Fashion Show," used here by special permission of Sears, Roebuck & Co.

It is an excellent guide to the planning, procedure and division of responsibility for the production of a fashion show. The example used here is from the retail level—but the guidelines apply to any level.

## YOU NEED A THEME

It is not enough just to collect a lot of clothes and parade them in front of an audience without rhyme or reason. They need to be held together by some fashion trend or style *theme.* This is your excuse for showing them at all. This is what you hang your advertising and

*Figure 73. Famous designers' shows draw buyers from all over the country and the world. Left: Oscar de la Renta shows a Spring Collection. Right: Kenzo shows his French Prêt-à-Porter collection to an international audience.*

your publicity on. According to its timeliness, interest and the effectiveness with which you *tell your story* (or detail your *theme*) your show will be successful or it will be a dismal failure. Themes are derived from many sources. Some of the obvious themes are: seasonal, special occasion, vacation and travel, entertainment, career fashions, active sports, new life styles.

## YOU NEED A COORDINATOR

The *Coordinator* is your key person. She must be endowed with fashion know-how, patience, tireless enthusiasm . . . and a *fashion show staff*. She must have a capacity for detail, and a willingness to take over practically any part of the job herself . . . from outfitting

200

a superstar fashion model to sweeping out the fitting room. If a firm does not have a staff fashion coordinator, then an outside specialist should be retained to work with management.

The Coordinator's major responsibilities are:

1. *Appointing her staff,* which should include someone from each of the apparel areas, to handle major garments—dresses, coats and suits, sports- and leisurewear—someone who will be responsible for all accessories; an alteration hand, several assistants to serve as dressing room workers, and someone who will be responsible for the pressing of the garments. In addition, the Advertising, Publicity and Display departments should be kept informed of the theme selected, colors to be featured, and all pertinent information.

2. *Developing the theme* in terms of actual merchandise.

3. *Discussing with the Buyer or Department Head* the merchandise which will be needed; he will have knowledge of what merchandise is on order, and when it will be in. If this does not cover the show's requirements, the department head should arrange for additional merchandise, in a range of colors and sizes, and should authorize withholding from stock merchandise already ordered.

4. *Arranging time and place* for fitting the models. There is always a room available somewhere in the store—not less than 20 feet square—where your racks, garments, alterations hand; models and coordinator can be centered. She will do the fitting in far less time, and do a better job.

5. *Working closely with the accessories representative* during the fittings. As the coordinator sees the garment on the model she can write out her suggestions for accessories, and the representative of the accessories departments can carry them out. It is important in accessorizing group showings that accessories be carefully selected to present a diversified accessory story.

6. *Keeping descriptive notes* for the commentary, to be written and delivered by herself, or by whoever has been selected as commentator.

7. *Making merchandise and model sequence charts* for rehearsal and show.

8. *Setting up rehearsal arrangements,* and acquainting each

committee member with his or her responsibilities. All models and assistants should be told the exact time and place of the rehearsal, and of the show and the approximate length of time their services will be required.

9. *Assigning a responsible person* to get the models on and off stage on time, to work as liaison between the commentator on stage and in the dressing room backstage.

10. *Arranging for music* for rehearsal and show.

## YOU NEED AN AUDIENCE

It is necessary to select just the right audience from the point of view of potential good customers for your fashions. You must also ensure that there will be a large enough attendance to make all the time and effort and expense worthwhile.

## YOU NEED A PLAN

Do not attempt a fashion show without a well-organized plan of what you are going to do every step of the way. This plan will include date, place, length of the show, its theme, how many models, who the audience will be, what merchandise will be shown, and so on.

LENGTH OF SHOW—This is important since it will determine the number of models you will need to show a predetermined number of garments.

*Generally speaking,* forty-five minutes should be the maximum length for a show. In this time you can show fifty to sixty garments depending on the number of models and their degree of proficiency.

AUDIENCE—If you are presenting the show under your own auspices, take all necessary steps to make sure you have a guaranteed audience. If a sponsoring group is involved they must guarantee a minimum audience.

## YOU NEED MERCHANDISE

All merchandise shown should fit into the theme of the show. For example, a show for "at home" fashions would not include swimsuits; but a show of travel fashions would. And these swimsuits would all be carefully accessorized with items from the proper departments.

*Figure 74. The fashion show in its most formal form has all the elements of any hit musical. This is an industrial or trade show produced by Deering Milliken. (Courtesy of Deering Milliken Inc.)*

## YOU NEED MODELS

Here are some possibilities: Professional models; former models; your own employees—you might have some who have had some instruction; your sponsoring group; design school students; college students; members of a local theatre groups; dance school students.

*How many models?* This is determined by the number of garments you plan to show. *Eight* is generally the minimum if you have professional models. Their sizes should be 9, 10, 11 and 12. If you are staging your style show for a group, such as a Woman's Club or PTA or Junior League, it is usually best to use members as models, as this guarantees greater interest, cooperation and attendance. Here you may wish to use twelve models in assorted sizes. A good size breakdown in a lineup of twelve models is: four juniors, sizes 9 and 11; six misses, sizes 10 and 12; one mature woman with an ample, well-proportioned figure; and one model in a half size. If children are included, the appropriately sized garments would be selected from those departments.

*Figure 75. The retail fashion show for store customers is an exciting way to launch Back-to-School. See the evident delight on the faces of this audience at Bloomingdale's, Short Hills, N.J. (Note the editorial tie-in with REDBOOK Magazine.)*

Models' height should be at least 5′ 5″ in their "stocking-feet" if garments are to be shown to advantage and with the least necessity for costly and time-consuming alterations. In working with volunteers from the sponsoring group try tactfully to select those with the best figures. But, if the first vice-president is so eager to model, accept her anyway.

## YOU NEED A BUDGET

It costs money to give a fashion show. Once you have been given the authority to *plan* (not *give*) a show, it is wise to set down on paper your estimate on what the show should cost. Get an OK on this figure from whoever will pay the bills. Use these items as a guide to total cost.

### YOU NEED STAGING

Some of the elements of successful staging are:

- A stage or ramp or runway
- Theatrical lighting
- Music
- Public address system
- Background displays (or scenery)
- Props

Your display personnel are the logical ones to be responsible for these items. If the show is in a store the display department may be recruited to plan and build the *stage* (or runway) so that the *dressing rooms* are easily accessible and so that the models can get to the stage and back to the dressing room with minimum confusion.

### YOU NEED DRESSING SPACE

Dressing space should be *sufficient* to accommodate the models who are wearing your fashions, and the "assistants" you have assigned to help them dress and change. It should have one or two *full-length mirrors,* plus other adequately lit mirrors where makeup may be applied and hair fixed. It should have racks for the garments you are going to show, as well as racks or hooks for the models' own clothing.

### YOU NEED A COMMENTARY

The coordinator may also be the commentator. And sometimes it is good to turn the commentary over to a local celebrity, such as the newspaper's fashion editor, or a personality from a local radio or television program. In this case the commentary is often supplied by the coordinator. Do not let the term "Commentary" scare you. And if *you* are delegated to be the commentator, take confidence from the following.

Every time you make a sale, you are telling your customer what a garment will do for her—where she can wear it—what its particular advantages are, from a style or care viewpoint. Your audience is that customer, multiplied by perhaps 200—or even 500. But the important thing for you to remember is that you are telling the story to a customer—not "making a speech" or striving to sound like fashion copy.

*Be prepared to "ad-lib"* some fashion gems, to fill in any pauses that might occur between models' appearances. Perhaps something about skirt lengths, or a color trend, etc.

### YOU NEED A PROGRAM

As soon as the model sequence has been made definite, you are ready to write up your program. This can be as simple as an 8½ × 11 sheet of paper, folded once, giving you four 8½ × 5½ "pages." Offset printed listings, with prices, are really sufficient.

Your sponsoring group may want to plan a more elaborate program, listing their committees and officers. You then give them the fashion listing information as early as you have it ready.

### YOU NEED A REHEARSAL

A run-through including all the people concerned with the show is absolutely necessary. In a show to be held in the store, it is obviously impractical to rip the departments apart to provide the space that will be used on the show night. However, the training room can be arranged to approximate the conditions. At this time, the listing sheet should be in everyone's possession. If there are any inconsistencies, or if a model finds she cannot make a change fast enough to meet the schedule (although this should all have been worked out previously) all these things now have a chance to be solved.

### YOU NEED PROMOTION . . . AND GOOD PUBLICITY . . .

Promotion includes: posters, invitations, and tickets. Publicity includes: advance announcement; stories of the show, the fashions, the designs, the personalities in the audience.

If you are putting on a fashion show, do not keep it a secret. Go after an *audience* aggressively.

## FASHION OFFICES

Fashion offices are often operated by manufacturers, stores, and resident buying offices. A fashion coordinator or director is responsible for the research and communication of fashion information. She presents fashion and color trends to come, based upon research, observation, and experience.

The fashion coordinator must also study consumer markets and consumer wants and needs; develop sources of fashion information; prepare written market reports and forecasts; establish fashion promotional programs; coordinate color, silhouette, fabric into exciting fashion stories; spot new items, resources, design ideas; coordinate merchandise groups and accessories; plan and conduct fashion shows and other special events; plan promotional material.

The fashion office is important to all levels of the fashion industry. It is the research and development department of a fashion firm.

## CONCLUSION

The fashion show is unique because it is alive and mobile. The audience is seeing fashion being worn by very attractive people who are evidently enjoying the appearance and feel of it. There is considerable difference in the way you see a modified tent dress on a window mannequin, and the way you see it flow through space as a model moves across a stage.

For those who work with, wear, and appreciate fashion—the fashion show can create magic. And this fashion show magic sells . . . it presents creative talent in textile and apparel design; introduces new expression; launches trends; suggests how to merchandise; influences customers to buy and generates fashion news which results in customer acceptance and response.

# 11

# Special Events and Features for Customer Involvement

SPECIAL EVENTS are specific devices, features, services, sales inducements, exhibits, demonstrations and attractions which are used to influence the sale of merchandise or ideas. In order to meet the growing competition in the fashion industry, firms have developed new methods of selling prospective purchasers. They have supplemented their advertising, publicity and display with other forms of sales promotion which we shall call special events.

Frequently two or more of the events may be used in combination. Sometimes, for example, a *merchandise* special event and an *institutional* special event may be combined by presenting an expert or consultant to give demonstrations of merchandise. Celebrities may be invited to appear as commentators or as models at fashion shows; or to serve on panels or as judges in customer or employee contests. Almost invariably, firms seek to obtain press publicity for their special displays and exhibits or other such merchandise and institutional special events. This is a very important objective of the special event. Many firms in the fashion business link their publicity and special events programs because of this close relationship. The following are five categories of special events used by producers and retailers in the fashion industry.

*Figure 76. It takes imagination and creative merchandising to develop so many special events out of the "Return of the Wok."*

1. *Merchandise Events*
   A. Product displays and exhibits
   B. Demonstrations and showings
   C. Schools and classes
2. *Institutional Events*
   A. Parades
   B. Shows (Fashion, Flower)
   C. Sponsorship of athletic teams (Bowling, Little League Baseball)
   D. Celebrity visits
   E. Lectures
   F. Consultants (Bridal, College)
3. *Free Samples of Merchandise*
4. *Special Sales Inducements*
   A. Premiums—(Special Offers)
   B. Special Conditions of Sale—(August Fur Lay-a-Way Sale)
   C. Contests (Customer and Employee)
   D. Giveaways—(Goodwill specialties, The Shopping Bag, Reuse Packaging)
5. *Customer Advisory Boards.* (Consumer Panels, College Boards, Career Boards)

## THE IMPORTANCE OF SPECIAL EVENTS

The special events used on each of the market levels differ widely in nature; but they all are used to accomplish one or more of several general sales objectives. When used by retail stores, they are expected to attract customer traffic—to draw large numbers of customers to the store where they will be exposed to the merchandise and ideas the store wants to sell. Stores in metropolitan locations use these events to attract customers to "come on downtown." The shopping centers and malls employ special events directors to plan activities designed to stimulate customer traffic.

Special events also serve to impress customers that a store is a community headquarters for a variety of educational and entertaining events. The special event endeavors to develop in customers, the habit of visiting the store regularly and often.

Manufacturers can use special events to accomplish the same objectives of increasing *showroom traffic and interest* in products

*Figure 77. This week at Bergdorf's is more than elegant fashion merchandise—it is stimulating special events to stimulate and involve its customers.*

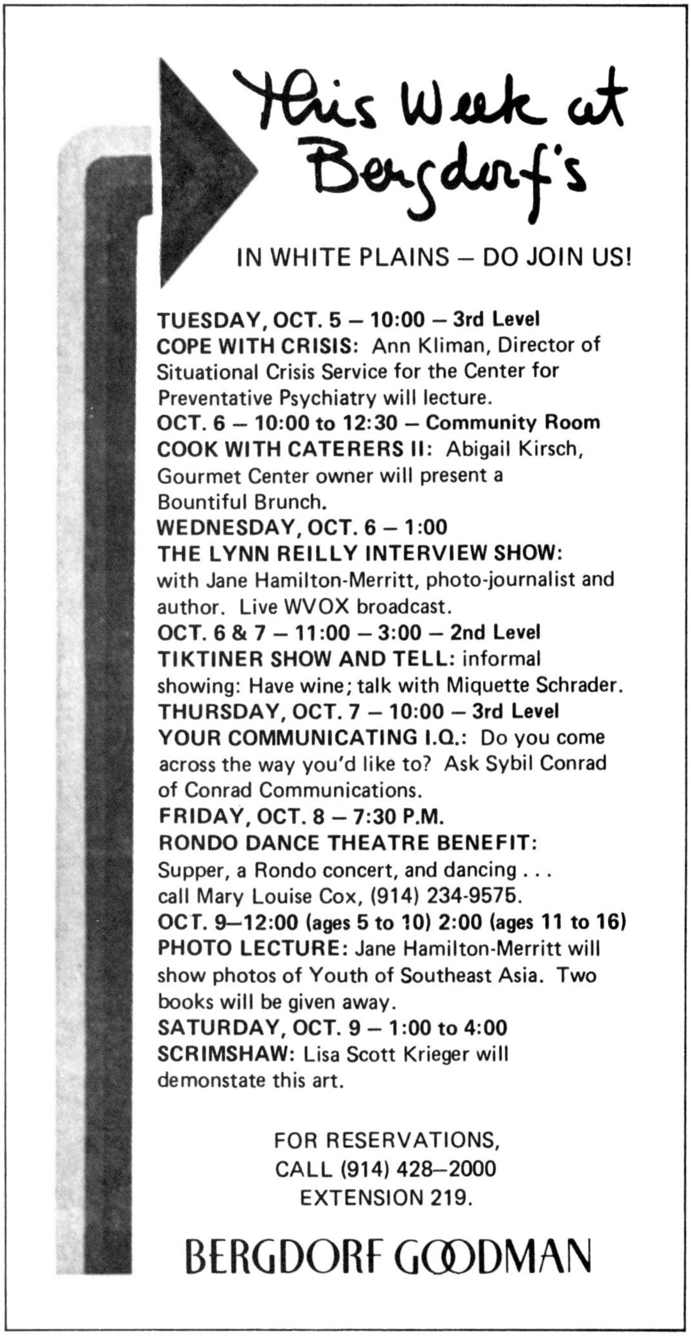

This Week at Bergdorf's

IN WHITE PLAINS — DO JOIN US!

**TUESDAY, OCT. 5 — 10:00 — 3rd Level**
**COPE WITH CRISIS:** Ann Kliman, Director of Situational Crisis Service for the Center for Preventative Psychiatry will lecture.
**OCT. 6 — 10:00 to 12:30 — Community Room**
**COOK WITH CATERERS II:** Abigail Kirsch, Gourmet Center owner will present a Bountiful Brunch.
**WEDNESDAY, OCT. 6 — 1:00**
**THE LYNN REILLY INTERVIEW SHOW:** with Jane Hamilton-Merritt, photo-journalist and author. Live WVOX broadcast.
**OCT. 6 & 7 — 11:00 — 3:00 — 2nd Level**
**TIKTINER SHOW AND TELL:** informal showing: Have wine; talk with Miquette Schrader.
**THURSDAY, OCT. 7 — 10:00 — 3rd Level**
**YOUR COMMUNICATING I.Q.:** Do you come across the way you'd like to? Ask Sybil Conrad of Conrad Communications.
**FRIDAY, OCT. 8 — 7:30 P.M.**
**RONDO DANCE THEATRE BENEFIT:** Supper, a Rondo concert, and dancing . . . call Mary Louise Cox, (914) 234-9575.
**OCT. 9—12:00 (ages 5 to 10) 2:00 (ages 11 to 16)**
**PHOTO LECTURE:** Jane Hamilton-Merritt will show photos of Youth of Southeast Asia. Two books will be given away.
**SATURDAY, OCT. 9 — 1:00 to 4:00**
**SCRIMSHAW:** Lisa Scott Krieger will demonstate this art.

FOR RESERVATIONS,
CALL (914) 428—2000
EXTENSION 219.

**BERGDORF GOODMAN**

Figure 78. Lord and Taylor celebrates its 150 years in fashion as a storewide event —Adventure 150. The ad above is a chronicle of those years.

and services they offer. They also use the event as an integral part of a program to obtain advantageous product and institutional publicity. Retailers have generally done more than fashion producers and apparel manufacturers to develop new and diversified special events because of their constant effort to keep customer traffic high and continuous.

## CONCLUSION

A few retailers have separated their effort into a separate *Special Events Division.* The responsibility for special events promotion as mentioned previously is sometimes combined with that of publicity. The size and diversity of a firm's special events program would determine whether it needs a separate department to handle it. As in the other sales promotion activities, advertising and sales promotion agencies, consultants and free-lance specialists are equipped to plan and to execute such events.

The current trend is to more community-oriented events, demonstrations and services. The big storewide event with its huge expense and long periods of planning have given way to smaller scale, more personalized departmental events.

*Figure 79. An effective special events connection—Macy's celebrates along with the nation with its own fireworks.*

# 12

## Personal Selling–
## The Bottom Line

PERSONAL SELLING is unquestionably the one activity that every
marketing or merchandising division must be concerned with year
after year. Personal selling seems to be the one function which most
sales managers admit is continually deteriorating. It is a problem at
every level of the industry. At the start of each planning period, sales
executives set objectives for increased sales, but too often they have
no answer to the question of *how*. This chapter offers no sure formula for effective personal selling, only some guidelines which
have helped.

One factor looms clear, however. Haphazard supervision and
management are generally behind poor selling. Sales training programs for sales personnel can be a key to the attainment of sales
objectives.

How often have you heard a customer (maybe yourself) leave a
retail store with the remark, "I'll never set foot in that store again!"
The point is that the salesperson represents the entire organization
to the customer. The customer has no other contact. It is not difficult to justify including this sort of "pointer" in any sales training
program.

A planned program of sales training is important to the success of
a business. All the activities which precede this chapter are of little

or no value to a company which fails in this one final activity, which some call the "moment of truth" in all marketing and merchandising—the *bottom line*. Whose job is sales personnel training and development? It is a shared responsibility.

Personnel divisions coordinate the program and provide basic training in procedures and policies; how to write up a sale—store policies with regard to services, returns, exchanges, guarantees, and other such basic knowledge. Experience on the selling floor is the responsibility of this division.

The promotion division plans and executes storewide promotions, sales campaigns, and programs in intensified efforts to supplement personal selling.

The merchandising division through its merchandise manager, but principally through buyers and assistant buyers, has a twofold responsibility. One is to inform the sales personnel about every item in the department. This means education in detail of what each product does or does not, its merits, its content, its benefits to the purchaser. The second is to share information and company objectives with salespeople.

## SHARING INFORMATION AND OBJECTIVES WITH SALESPEOPLE

The responsibility of marketing and merchandising executives does not stop with planning, buying, and promotion. While many newer retail organization charts distinctly separate buying from selling, these two functions had better be well coordinated, if the sweet taste of sales success is to be realized.

Smart merchandising executives will regularly find time to be on the selling floor, or in the case of wholesalers, in the selling field. That is where almost everything of importance to sales volume really happens. It is there that reactions and impressions can be experienced firsthand. A piece of paper can be dull and rather lifeless. There is no substitute for person-to-person relationships.

The reaction of any one customer is important, but experiences with many customers are incomparable.

The merchandiser must have had a reason for buying any specific item. That reason should be given to the store salespeople who meet the customers. A written memorandum has its limitations. It can

*Figure 80. Rich's of Atlanta uses special events to involve customers. The cooking class and exercise demonstration were part of an in-store GLAMOUR Magazine Workshop for young career women.*

216

rarely stimulate excitement. On the other hand, it is wise to support a personal sales meeting with a written summary of the important points made at the meeting.

In every area of communication, it is agreed that better transmission of message results from arousing as many senses as possible. The subsequent memorandum serves to assist the memory factor.

Meetings with salespeople need not be dull nor should the meeting be conducted in a monotone. Enthusiasm and boredom are both contagious. One just happens to be better than the other. Buyers and merchandisers who feel that a particular item may be difficult to present with enthusiasm, might well consider *not* buying that item. Customers might feel the same way about it. This is no proposal for a false or phony presentation of merchandise, for that becomes obvious. Salespeople have instincts, and meetings should not be held unnecessarily, nor be conducted at the same pitch for every session or for every item.

Once sales personnel *know* the whats and whys of merchandise, then coordination of effort can get to work and produce results.

Meetings should not be conducted when the listeners leave with the-same-old-stuff impression. Presentation should be honest and genuine. The ability to stimulate sales effort is in itself an art.

## CUSTOMER FEEDBACK

The exchange of ideas and information must work two ways: From the executive to the sales staff and in the reverse direction also. Salespeople can be a vital listening post for merchandisers and promotional executives.

Salespeople should be encouraged to listen to the customers; to what they like; what they do not like; to their objections and to their requests. These findings should be reported *in writing* to merchandising staff. Verbal reports are too easily forgotten. Such reports should be sources for action and consideration. Considerable buying sense is often developed by such practices. Buying sense translates into promotional direction quite often.

## PERSONAL SELLING ON THE RETAIL LEVEL

PERSONAL SELLING IS DEFINED AS—An oral presentation in conversation with a prospective customer for the purpose of making a sale of merchandise, services or ideas. The following will concern personal selling on the retail level at the point-of-sale. The techniques discussed are generally applicable to other market levels.

There are two types of retail selling in current practice. These are: *simplified selling* and *personalized salesmanship.* Simplified selling is a general term that is currently used to describe the various methods of *putting the customer in more direct contact* with mer-

Figure 81. Stars from the musical show "Bubbling Brown Sugar" were invited to Burdines, Miami, for demonstrations of Fashion Fair's new line, "Bubbling Brown Sugar."

chandise. It is sometimes called *self-service.* This method reduces, or in some cases eliminates a number of salespeople. Personalized salesmanship implies the situation in which a salesperson initiates the customer's contact with the merchandise and *completes the sale.*

Each of these two types has inherent advantages and disadvantages. The advantages of simplified selling are:

1. *It reduces the retailer's selling cost*—Many stores which feature low-price merchandise and work on lower margin find simplified selling is a necessity.
2. *It is more efficient* for certain types of retail operations which feature certain categories of merchandise. For example, merchandise which is already packaged, and pre-sold through extensive sales promotion.
3. *It is actually preferred by many customers*—Self-service is a retailing way of life today.

Personalized selling has these advantages:

1. *Some customer groups prefer* personal attention and service. They are interested in counsel and advice. They want someone to answer their questions, demonstrate features and suggest uses.
2. *Salespeople may suggest additional merchandise* and make "extra" sales more efficiently than self-service fixtures can. Salespeople can explain merchandise features that are not always too obvious by demonstrating the merchandise in use. Salespeople can complete sales that have been initiated by other sales promotion activities, such as display, advertising, publicity, special events and fashion shows.

## WHAT IS SALESMANSHIP?

The purpose of salesmanship is to help customers to buy what they want and that which will give them satisfaction. The experienced salesperson will not be passive in his approach to his customer's wants. He presents selling points and appeals which are designed to stimulate those wants. He is prepared to make suggestions to customers who are not sure what they want. He is also ready to "service" those customers who come to the point-of-sale with a fixed idea of what they want. The effective salesperson does not persuade customers to buy what they do not really want.

## IMPORTANCE OF SALESMANSHIP
## FOR FASHION MERCHANDISE

Many businesses are asking today: "Are salespeople necessary? How much personal selling does my business need? What 'sales promotion mix' do I use—heavy advertising, display, and self-service with light personal selling or vice versa?" There is no simple answer to these questions. Any form of selling involves a *selling and buying process.* This process, (previously mentioned as the *AIDA procedure*), can be implemented entirely by personal selling—or in *part* by personal selling. The other sales promotion activities can bring the customer to the "last three feet" up to the point-of-sale. Advertising, publicity and display may have pre-sold this customer. In some cases, all the salesperson has to do is close the sale. It is the nature of a business, the character of its merchandise and the class of its customers which determine the "sales promotion mix."

## THE SELLING PROCESS—AIDA (AGAIN)

1. Get *Attention* of customers.
2. Create *Interest and Desire* for product or service that is being offered.
3. Stimulate to *Action*—Get customer to buy.
4. Customer *Satisfaction*—To avoid returns and assure repeated patronage.

## WHAT SALESPEOPLE MUST KNOW

1. Know their product and understand its important qualities of the merchandise from customers' viewpoint.
2. Know customers and what they expect from salespeople, e.g., service and/or information and/or advice.
3. Know what is in stock in order to find it quickly.
4. Understand today's customers—educated, affluent, impulse buyers who are too busy to waste time. They know what they want, have relatively little store "loyalties," switch brands easily. They are too sophisticated to be talked into merchandise that they do not want. The philosophy of "Caveat Emptor" (let the buyer beware) is being challenged by the current "the consumer is king."

5. Understand the retailer's viewpoint—"The customer is always right."

# SOME GENERAL PRINCIPLES OF SALESMANSHIP

## PERSONAL SELLING TECHNIQUES

1. The customer's viewpoint is the primary consideration in selling procedure. The salesperson is well advised to tell customers those things which they want most to hear about the merchandise. Listening to and observing the customer's interest can guide this step.
2. Customers should be given reasons why they should buy. They want to be told, "What will it do for me?"
3. The selling conversation should avoid the mechanical and obvious. The canned pitch is not acceptable to today's customers.
4. Customers should not be "typed," in terms of price, probable intentions to buy, and the like.
5. The truth is still the best basis for any communication. It should be used in personal selling.

## APPROACHES—MEETING THE CUSTOMER
## (GETTING HER ATTENTION AND INTEREST,
## AND ACKNOWLEDGING HER ARRIVAL)

Of the main approaches, the greeting and the merchandise approach, the merchandise approach is generally more effective in getting customer's attention and arousing her interest. This involves an opening which mentions merchandise of interest to the customer.

Approaches which can too easily bring forth a negative response, such as, "May I help you?" make it too easy to say "No." A simple greeting, such as "Good morning," is preferable.

## DETERMINING CUSTOMER'S NEEDS AND
## WANTS TO AROUSE INTEREST

1. The salesperson should be alert to the customer's reactions to merchandise.
2. The salesperson should listen to what the customer has said and is saying.

3. The salesperson should ask a minimum of questions, (e.g., it is unwise to ask the price that the customer wants to spend).

## PRESENTATION OF MERCHANDISE AND DEVELOPMENT OF SELLING POINTS

A process of show and tell to create interest and stimulate desire.

1. Merchandise should be presented as promptly as possible.
2. The customer is impressed when salespeople handle merchandise with appreciation.
3. The customer is confused by being shown an "excessive" amount of merchandise.
4. The salesperson should start by showing medium-priced merchandise from which he can trade-up or down, depending on customer's reactions.
5. Merchandise should be shown in use whenever appropriate.
6. An appeal to the customer's senses should be attempted. Customer should be encouraged to touch and handle merchandise.

## GIVE SELLING POINTS SIMULTANEOUSLY WITH PRESENTATION TO CREATE DESIRE

1. A customer should be told first what she most wants to hear about merchandise.
2. The salesperson should give *reasons to buy* by telling her "what it will do for her."
3. The salesperson should emphasize those qualities which are most desirable from the customer's point-of-view (e.g., suitability, utility, economy, variety of uses). Too many points, however, will confuse a customer.
4. The positive should be emphasized with benefits highlighted.

## MEETING AND OVERCOMING OBJECTIONS (IF ANY)

Some common objections by customers are: resistance to price, requests for out-of-stock items, just-looking, indecision and so on.

Some recognized techniques for overcoming objections are:

1. Answer objections before they are raised by watching customer's reactions.
2. Do *not* argue with customer.
3. Admit objections and point out a superior feature.

## STIMULATING ACTION TO BUY—"CLOSING THE SALE"

1. Cease showing additional merchandise.
2. Narrow the selection and concentrate on those items in which customer shows great interest. Remove others.
3. Use stimulators which can produce a decision:
   A. Present alternatives, e.g., "Which do you prefer?"
   B. Suggest decision, e.g., "Do you wish to charge this?"
   C. Assume decision, e.g., "You've made a wise choice."

The salesperson should avoid high-pressuring and hurrying the customer before she is ready.

## SUGGESTION SELLING

*Suggestion is not substitution*—It is a method of increasing a sale by:

1. Suggesting related merchandise.
2. Suggesting larger quantities of same merchandise.
3. Suggesting "specials" and/or advertised merchandise.

Suggestions can be made more emphatic by showing the merchandise rather than asking if the customer would ". . . like to see something else."

# CONCLUSION

The sales promotion problem of all firms on all market levels is fundamentally similar. Each business has the individual problems of defining its own objectives and policies; determining the class of customer it can serve best; deciding upon the character and extent of the merchandise and services it will offer; selecting the forms and media for sales promotion, which will do the best job of attracting and selling customers.

It is difficult sometimes to distinguish the specific characteristics which make one firm superior to another. Yet, no business can achieve any great success unless its performance is either different or better in some way than its competition. The purpose of sales promotion is to communicate with customers and make them aware of the better job a firm is doing for them. A business must differentiate its value to its customers, and then with stimulating and informative sales promotion, keep this impression going strong.

# Bibliography

The following list of books is considered by the authors to be especially helpful to instructors and students of fashion merchandising, advertising and promotion. It can serve as an additional source for the instructor's development of course and curriculum subject matter and instructional exercises. These selections also consider the specific needs of students who wish to supplement their readings of particular topics discussed in this book.

Abrahams, Howard P. *Making TV Pay Off: A Retailer's Guide To Television Advertising.* New York: Fairchild Publications, 1975.

Boucher, Francois. *20,000 Years of Fashion.* New York: Harry N. Abrams, Inc., 1967.

Burton, Philip Ward. *Advertising Copywriting.* 3rd ed. Columbus, Ohio: Grid, Inc. 1974.
_____. *Retail Advertising for The Small Store.* Englewood Cliffs, New Jersey: Prentice-Hall, Inc., 1959.

Cutlip, Scot. M., and Allen H. Center. *Effective Public Relations.* 4th ed. Englewood Cliffs, New Jersey: Prentice-Hall, Inc., 1971.

Diehl, Mary Ellen. *How To Produce A Fashion Show.* New York: Fairchild Publications, 1976.

Dunn, Watson S., and A.M. Barban. *Advertising: Its Role in Modern Marketing.* New York: Holt, Rinehart & Winston, 1974.

Edwards, Charles M. Jr., and Russel A. Brown. *Retail Advertising and Sales Promotion.* 3rd ed. Englewood Cliffs, New Jersey: Prentice-Hall, Inc., 1959.

Gold, Annalee. *How To Sell Fashion.* 2nd ed. New York: Fairchild Publications, 1978.
_____. *75 Years of Fashion.* New York: Fairchild Publications, 1975.

Gore, Bud. *How To Sell The Whole Store As Fashion.* New York: National Retail Merchants Association, 1970.

Haight, William. *Retail Advertising: Management and Techniques.* Morristown, New Jersey: General Learning Press, 1976.

Jarnow, Jeannette A., and Beatrice Judelle. *Inside The Fashion Business: Text and Readings.* 2nd ed. New York: John Wiley & Sons, Inc., 1974.

Joel, Shirley. *Fairchild's Book of Window Display.* New York: Fairchild Publications, 1973.

Kleppner, Otto, and Stephen Greysen. *Advertising Procedure.* 6th ed. New York: Englewood Cliffs, New Jersey: Prentice-Hall, Inc., 1973.

McLuhan, Marshall. *Understanding Media: The Extensions of Man.* New York: McGraw-Hill, Inc., 1964.

Milton, Shirley. *Advertising Copywriting.* Dobbs Ferry, New York: Oceana Publications, 1969.

———. *Advertising for Modern Retailers.* New York: Fairchild Publications, 1975.

National Retail Merchants Association. *How To Profit from Retail Radio Advertising.* New York: 1975.

———. *Visual Merchandising.* New York: 1974.

Ocko, Judy Young, and M.L. Rosenblum. *The Secret Ingredient of Good Retail Ads: A Handbook for Buyers and Their Bosses.* New York: National Retail Merchants Association, 1974.

Packard, Sidney, Arthur A. Winters, and Nathan Axelrod. *Fashion Buying and Merchandising.* New York: Fairchild Publications, 1977.

Packard, Sidney, and Abraham Raine. *Consumer Behavior and Fashion Marketing.* Dubuque, Iowa: Kendall/Hunt Publishing Co., 1977.

Rosenblum, M.L. *How To Design Effective Store Advertising.* Rev. ed. New York: National Retail Merchants Association, 1974.

Stone, Bob. *Successful Direct Marketing Methods.* Chicago, Illinois: Crain Books, 1974.

Wright, John S., D.S. Warner, and W.L. Winter. *Advertising.* 3rd ed. New York: McGraw-Hill, Inc., 1971.

# Glossary

The following is a list of selected terms with definitions drawn from authoritative sources and from acceptance in the industry. In some instances, explanation may go beyond definition, and usage may be further indicated.

**A.A.A.A.** *(American Association of Advertising Agencies)* The four A's. The national organization of advertising agencies.

**A.B.C.** *(Audit Bureau of Circulation)* Organization sponsored by publications and by agencies to secure and publish verified circulation statements. See *Circulation.*

**ACCOUNT EXECUTIVE** Member of agency staff who is the liaison between the client (advertiser) and the agency. Keeps aware of advertiser's plans and needs; carries this data to agency personnel; then brings agency plans to advertiser.

**ADVERTISING** Any paid, nonpersonal message by an identified sponsor; appears in media and used to influence sales, services, or the acceptance of ideas by potential buyers.

**ADVERTISING AGENCY** An organization which renders advertising (and marketing) services to clients.

**ADVERTISING ALLOWANCE** Money paid by a primary producer to a wholesaler or retailer or from a wholesaler to a retailer for the specific purpose of contributing to the advertising of a brand or product, most often for consumer advertising. See *Cooperative Advertising.*

**ADVERTISING BUDGET** A plan of advertising expenditures for a specified period: weekly, monthly, seasonally or annually. Generally details by media and by departments or divisions.

**ADVERTISING CAMPAIGN** Series of advertising messages devoted to a single theme, concept or idea with a definite objective.

ADVERTISING DIRECTOR The person in charge of personnel and activities of the advertising department. Sometimes display and publicity are included in his responsibilities.

ADVERTISING MATRIX *(Newspaper Ad Mat)* Mold of paper pulp or similar material made by pressing sheet of the substance into metal type or engraving plate. Forms a replica of the original plate (stereotype) for printing process.

ADVERTISING REQUEST *(Buyer's Information Form)* Department store buyer's form to order advertising space. Submitted to advertising department with all pertinent information of merchandise to be advertised.

ADVERTISING SCHEDULE The plan of timing, media, amount of space, and items to be advertised for specified period.

AGATE LINE Unit of measure in newspaper printed space. It is one column wide, regardless of width, and always one-fourteenth of an inch deep. (Fourteen agate lines deep to the column inch.)

AGENCY COMMISSION Compensation paid by a medium to agencies for services in placement of advertising. Usually 15 percent discount of space cost for prompt payment; sometimes passed on to client or retained by agency, depending upon agreement between agency and client.

ALLOCATION Percentage of appropriation which is assigned to activity, media, divisions or departments.

AM *(Amplitude Modulation)* The standard broadcast transmission system of majority of licensed radio stations. Used to differentiate from FM.

A.N.P.A. *(American Newspaper Publishers' Association)* Major trade association of daily and Sunday newspapers.

APPEAL Motive to which advertising is directed, designed to stimulate action by the audience. Points made in copy to meet customers' needs and objectives, and provide reasons to buy.

APPROACH Manner of presentation of appeals as determined by copywriter. Can be factual, imaginative or combination of the two.

APPROPRIATION In sales promotion, the dollars designated for all promotion activities. It is usually 1% to 4% of annual gross volume.

ARBITRON 1. Device for producing instant electronic television program ratings. 2. Name of the service which places the unit in households.

ART An element of print advertising. Includes photography, wash illustrations or line drawings.

AUDIENCE People reached by an advertising medium.

AUDIENCE COMPOSITION The number of people reached by advertising according to age, sex, income, home, etc. Also known as audience profile.

AUDIENCE CUME *(Cumulative)* For *radio* and *television,* the total number of different people reached by a station in two or more time periods, or the net (unduplicated) audience in a specified span of time. For *newspapers,* the number of different people reached in a time period. All media usually measured by the week.

AUDIENCE PROFILE See *Audience Composition.*

AUDIENCE RATING Proportion of total homes reached in a market area of those residential units equipped with radios, or television sets, for a given period of time. Degree of penetration of a station or program to those homes.

AUDIENCE SURVEY Market study measuring number of homes in an audience. Accomplished by aided recall, interview or meter techniques.

AUDIO In television, the sound part of a broadcast.

BALANCE, FORMAL Used in advertising layout and in display when a dominant point of interest is desired with subordinate elements to develop equal attention power.

BALANCE, INFORMAL Attention is gained by dynamic balance in arrangement of elements. Difference in attention power caused by shape, color or arrangement, often with dissimilar units.

BASE RATE See *Open Rate.*

BLACK AND WHITE *(B/W)* Printing on white paper with black ink (or vice versa). No color is used. Also known as monotone.

BODY COPY The main paragraph(s) of copy in an advertisement.

BOLD-FACED TYPE Style of darker, heavier type; bolder and thicker than regular type.

BRAND Name on identifying label of a seller, usually promoted in advertising to achieve customer recognition and preference.

BROADSIDE Promotion piece of one large sheet of paper, usually printed on one side. As the paper is unfolded, so is the message.

BROCHURE Elaborate folder or booklet.

BUDGET The determined sum to be spent on sales promotion; apportioned to planned activities, segmented and detailed under general allocations.

BULK RATES Reductions in cost of space or time with benefits in cost for use and frequency, offered by media to advertisers.

CAPTION Headline of an advertisement, or descriptive matter accompanying an illustration or a publicity release.

CAR CARD Poster-like designed card, usually placed in buses or subways. Common sizes are 11″ high and 28″, 42″, or 56″ long. The 11″ height is standard for such cards.

CENTER SPREAD Two facing pages in centerfold of a newspaper or magazine. See *Spread*.

CIRCULATION In *print,* number of copies of a vehicle, based on a number of issues. In *broadcast,* number of households tuned in over an extended period (week or month). In *outdoor,* the number of people who pass a billboard in a day. See *A.B.C.* and *Controlled Circulation*.

CLASSIFIED ADVERTISING Notices and advertising grouped by classifications under headings without illustrations except when sold as "display classified." Sold by the line or by the number of words.

COLOR Sold in printing, art, photography, television. As opposed to black/white, more expensive and more involved in production; more realistic. Proven to have greater selling impact. See *Four-color Process* and *Spot Color*.

COLD TYPE Type set by typewriter or by electronic or photographic process, not using molten metal. Used in lithographic (offset) printing and often now in letter-press.

COLUMN INCH Space one column wide and one inch deep (regardless of the width of the column). Most common measuring unit in newspaper advertising.

COMMERCIAL Advertising message on radio or television. Also known as a spot or announcement. Often abused by announcer in a program who introduces the message as "a *word* from the sponsor."

COMMUNICATIONS The process of sending and receiving messages. In *marketing,* these messages must go in both directions as a mutual process.

COMPARISON OFFICE A staff used to check local competition for prices, assortments, service. Found only in larger retail stores.

COMPOSITION The setting and arranging of copy in type.

CONSUMER Ultimate user of a product.

CONTINUITY Repetition of effective characteristics in advertising; a factor of frequency that establishes buyer recognition of an organization and its products.

CONTROLLED CIRCULATION Distribution of printed advertising media such as free newspapers, shopping guides, magazines. Selected distribution in an area. See *Circulation*.

COOPERATIVE ADVERTISING Advertising run by a local advertiser in conjunction with a national advertiser. Cost is shared. National advertiser generally provides newspaper ad mats (matrix). Names of participants appear in the advertisement.

COPY All the words in an advertisement. Some define this as *any* material used in an advertisement.

COPY PLATFORM 1. Statement of basic ideas for a campaign or an advertisement with selling points in descending order of importance. 2. Statement of advertising policy as instructions to agency or to copywriters.

COPY STRATEGY Entire plan for effective advertising with statement of objectives of an advertisement, usually applied to a campaign or series of advertisements.

COPYRIGHT Legal protection presumably afforded to authors of original artistic or intellectual works.

COPYWRITER The writer of wording in advertising, often the originator of concept.

COVERAGE Number of homes or persons exposed to a broadcast medium within a specified time or exposed to an issue of print medium. Generally a percentage of entire group that can be reached.

CPM *(Cost per Thousand)* Used in comparing media costs. Interpreted as cost per thousand readers or listeners or viewers.

CREDITS, EDITORIAL In *publicity,* the listing of retail outlets where merchandise may be purchased. Includes the names of designer, manufacturer; type of fabric; supplier of coordinating accessories.

CROP Trimming of illustration to eliminate nonessential background or of detail to fit desired allocated space.

CUME See *Audience Cume.*

CUSTOMER PROFILE Statement of demographic characteristics of people considered to be prospects for a given product(s) or of people who shop in a given area.

CUT 1. In *print,* a plate or engraving of pictorial or illustrative material. See *Photoengraving.* In *broadcast,* an abrupt change from one scene to another. 2. Used as a term to "eliminate," or to "conclude."

DEALER IMPRINT A retailer's name imprinted, pasted on, or rubber stamped in space provided on literature supplied by manufacturer.

DEALER TIE-IN 1. The association of a local dealer's advertising with national advertising. 2. Promotional materials supplied to a dealer to identify with a national campaign.

DEMOGRAPHICS Vital statistics of a population segment. Based on sex, age, education, religion, race, family size, type of home, income, life style.

DIRECT ADVERTISING Any printed advertising distributed directly to specific prospects by mail, by salespeople, or by dealers; not through paid media.

DISPLAY *(Visual Merchandising)* Nonpersonal physical presentation of merchandise or ideas. Can be window, exterior, interior, or remote.

DISPLAY ADVERTISING Printed advertising which contains headlines, body copy, illustrations . . . some or all of these elements.

DRIVE TIME Hours of the day when most people drive to or from work. In most instances, 7 to 9 A.M. and 4 to 6:30 P.M.

EDITING Review, correction, and (ideally) improvement in copy. Also selection of scenes from television film or tape for final inclusion or deletion.

EFFECTIVE CIRCULATION 1. The number of people in a total circulation who can be considered as potential customers for a specific advertising offer. 2. The number of people who can be reasonably expected to view a poster or billboard, usually defined as one-half the pedestrians or automobiles and one-fourth the passengers on public surface transportation passing a given point.

ENGRAVING See *Photoengraving.*

EXCLUSIVE *(In A Press Release)* Indication that only one publication is receiving this story in an area.

EXTERIOR DISPLAY *(Facade)* Display on the store building or street. Flags, awnings, lights, bunting, potted trees, flowers are used to promote seasonal themes and special events.

FACADE See *Exterior Display.*

FACTUAL APPROACH Practical or rational presentation of appeals and selling points in advertising.

FASHION OFFICE Department in larger retail stores where fashion planning and fashion coordination between departments is centralized.

FASHION SHOW See *Show* and *Showing.*

FEDERAL COMMUNICATIONS COMMISSION *(FCC)* Federal agency empowered to license radio and television stations and to assign wave lengths.

FEDERAL TRADE COMMISSION *(FTC)* Federal agency empowered to prevent unfair competition, fraudulent or misleading advertising or deception in advertising among interstate trading companies.

FLYER Circular or announcement; generally printed on one side.

FM *(Frequency Modulation)* Transmission of radio signals by varying frequency of electromagnetic waves. Relatively short in reach area, but eliminates static. Sound reproduction is superior to AM.

FOLDER Printed circular, folded and often used as a mailing piece.

FORMAT In *print,* the shape, style, size, and appearance of a publication. In *broadcast,* the character of programming of a radio or television station; news, country music, rock, classical, talk, or ethnic programming.

FOUR-COLOR PROCESS Photoengraving procedure for reproducing color illustrations. This is done by a set of plates known as process plates; each prints one color: yellow, blue (cyan), red (magenta), black. The sequence varies, but together they produce full color printing.

FREQUENCY The number of exposures to a person or household of the message of an advertiser in a given period.

FRINGE TIME The hour before and the hour after prime time.

GLOSSY Photograph with a shiny surface or finish, necessary for reproduction in print.

GRAPHICS Illustrations, art, diagrams, charts.

GRAVURE Any of the processes of printing from a metal intaglio plate, as distinct from letterpress printing. See *Intaglio Printing.*

GROSS RATING POINTS (GRP) A measure of the total gross weight delivered by a TV or radio program or a spot schedule. GRP is the *sum of the ratings* for individual spots or programs, because *a rating point* indicates an audience of one percent of the coverage base. Example: 150 gross rating points means 1.5 messages per average home. See *Radio Rating Points.*

GUTTER Normally, the vertical unprinted area between facing pages and beyond copy and illustration. See *Spread.*

HALFTONE Photoengraving plate photographed through a glass screen in the camera. Breaks up the reproduction of the subject into dots (or screen), making possible the printing of shaded values, as in a photograph or wash illustration.

HEADLINE Major copy caption above text. The most important copy element in print advertising; usually, largest display type in ad.

HOT TYPE Metal printing type which when cooled is used for letterpress printing.

HOUSE BRAND Merchandise which bears a retailer's own name brand rather than that of a manufacturer. Also known as private brand or store brand.

I.D. (Pronounced EYE-DEE) Identification of advertiser in broadcast commercial. This usually refers to a ten-second spot.

IMAGE Real or imaginary impression of the public of a product brand, or the reputation of an organization.

IMAGINATIVE APPROACH In copy, the emotional presentation of appeals through the use of either projective or narrative writing. Not factual in development.

INSERT Special page(s) printed on better or different paper; either loose within a publication or bound in. Usually used for distinctive color work.

INSTITUTIONAL ADVERTISING Used to build and to maintain a company's reputation; to keep customers sold over extended periods on policies, services, merchandise.

INTAGLIO PRINTING *(Gravure)* Printing from depressed surfaces as on a copper or steel plate. Rotogravure is a form of intaglio printing used for some newspaper magazine supplements. Engraved announcements, documents, maps and currency are printed by this method.

INTERIOR DISPLAY (Departmental) In retail stores, display in departments, on counters, in glass cases, in aisles, on ledges, walls, columns, shadow boxes.

ITALIC TYPE Style in which the letters *slant* to the right.

KEYNOTE The basic idea or main appeal of an advertisement or promotion.

LAYOUT A working drawing which shows how advertisement will look with all the elements of the ad in position; a guide to those who work on copy, art and production.

LEAD In a news story or press release, the opening or introductory sentence(s). If no more than the lead were published, essence of story would be expressed. Contains the "5W's": who, what, when, where, why.

LETTERPRESS Printing from a raised (or relief) surface. Ink comes in contact with raised elements and in direct contact with paper, similar to a rubber stamp.

LEVELS OF SELLING Determined by who (which market level) is selling what to whom. Levels are: trade, national, retail.

LINEAGE A newspaper designation to denote the number of agate lines in an advertisement or in a schedule. Also may refer to "national lineage" or "retail lineage," or a segment such as "automotive lineage."

LINE DRAWING Illustration made with pen, pencil, brush or crayon for print advertising, composed of lines or crosshatch lines in imitation of shading. Variation in tone is indicated only by the width of the lines.

LITHOGRAPHY (Offset) Printing from a level or flat surface on which non-printing areas are chemically treated to repel ink and to attract water. Ink and water are spread on plate from respective "fountains" while press runs. Thin and flexible plates are used to "offset" the image to a rubber blanket, which then transfers the image to paper.

LOCAL ADVERTISING That which is placed and paid for by the retailer or local dealer as opposed to national advertising which is paid for by a manufacturer. In radio or television, it is exposure to a local audience in contrast to network or national exposure.

LOCAL RATE That cost of advertising space or time which is restricted to local (retail) merchants and is lower than the national rate.

LOGOTYPE *(Logo)* Trademark or signature of product or company in a distinctive lettering or design. Example: The CBS "eye."

MAIL-ORDER ADVERTISING Method of selling in which entire transaction is handled by advertising and ordered by mail. No salesperson is involved. Can also be ordered by phone.

MANNEQUIN A model form of a full or part of a human figure; used in display.

MARKDOWN Reduction in selling price to encourage buying.

MARKET Any group with the desire and ability to buy.

MARKET LEVEL Determined by position of company in the marketing process: raw material producer (primary); finished product manufacturer (secondary); retailer (retail). Levels are: primary, secondary, and retail.

MARKET PROFILE The demographic description of the people, households, or groups to be considered prospects for a product or group of products. Prospects may be segmented as to primary to secondary.

MARKETING Total research, development, planning, pricing, distribution, promotional activities involved in moving goods and services from producer to seller to consumer. Total marketing requires integration of all these activities.

MARKETING STRATEGY The plan for marketing as adopted.

MASS MEDIUM A channel for advertising that appeals to great numbers of diverse groups of people. Not beamed to a selected audience or *class* medium.

MATRIX See *Advertising Matrix.*

MECHANICAL All elements of an advertisement, proofs of type and illustrations, photos, etc. pasted in final arrangement (usually on artboard), ready for camera. Photography is then used to make printing plate.

MEDIA MIX The plan of a promotion which segments for maximum effect, amount of space and/or time to be used in each medium. It apportions exposure to print (newspapers, magazines, mailings), radio, television.

MEDIA STUDY OR RESEARCH Analysis of audience and coverage of various media with objective of effective selection and economical buying for desired results.

MEDIUM 1. The singular form of media. The channel that carries advertising: newspaper, magazine, radio, television, outdoor (billboard), transit sign, direct mail, etc. 2. The material used by an artist such as pen and ink, pencil, wash, crayon, photography.

MERCHANDISE-ACCEPTANCE CURVE An attempt to visualize a product's position in public acceptance at a given time. It is not a measurement of this acceptance, but rather an estimate of rising, continuing, or declining customer preference.

MERCHANDISE MANAGER The executive who supervises a group of store buyers (not consumers). The General Merchandise Manager supervises and coordinates the work of the Divisional Merchandise Managers.

MERCHANDISING 1. The buying and selling functions of a retailer designed to present the right product, at the right time, at the right price. 2. Many manufacturers use this term to describe the promotion of their advertising to their sales force, wholesalers, and retailers.

MILLINE RATE The factor in comparison of newspaper costs. It is the cost of one agate line per million circulation. Computed by multiplying the line rate by one million, then dividing by the circulation. The million figure has been established as standard and convenient.

MONOTONE See *Black and White.*

MOTIVATION Similar to motive, but refers to the stimulus which initiates a motive.

MOTIVATIONAL RESEARCH Psychological studies to probe basic conscious and unconscious reasons for buying habits. Respondents speak freely in this type of study. Questionnaires are not used. The method is unstructured.

MOTIVE Some inner drive, impulse, intention that causes a person to do something or to act in a certain way.

N.A.B. *(Newspaper Advertising Bureau)* Collects and prepares information about newspapers, rates, circulation data.

NATIONAL ADVERTISING Advertising by a primary producer or a secondary manufacturer as opposed to that of a local retailer. National advertising is not necessarily a matter of geography or national coverage.

NATIONAL BRAND See *Brand.* Manufacturer's brand with wide distribution, as distinguished from "private brand."

NETWORK Group of interconnecting radio or television stations for simultaneous broadcasts.

NIELSEN The A.C. Nielsen Company provides and takes audience measurements for network programs (N.S.I.—Nielsen Station Index; N.T.I.—Nielsen Television Index).

OFFSET See *Lithography.*

ONE-TIME RATE See *Open Rate.*

OPEN RATE The highest advertising rate upon which all discounts are based. Also called base rate or one-time rate.

OUTDOOR ADVERTISING Signs, posters, billboards placed out of doors, on sides of building, on billboards, on roofs, along railroads.

OVERLAPPING CIRCULATION Duplication of distribution when two or more media are used. Often more effective for additional impact.

P.A. Public Address System. Amplification method for sound by use of microphone(s) and electronic speakers.

PACKAGE 1. The wrapper on a product or a container. 2. A show or series of shows bought by an advertiser usually for a lump sum, to include all components.

PASTE-UP See *Mechanical.*

PENETRATION Percentage of total households or homes owning at least one television set reached in a specified area.

PERCENTAGE OF SALES BUDGETING Promotional budgets are prepared based on *anticipated* sales for the period of the budget. The estimate of anticipated sales is based on past performances *and* prospects for the forthcoming period.

PERSONAL SELLING Oral presentation (in conversation) with a prospective customer.

PHOTOENGRAVING The metal form from which an advertisement can be printed. Also known as engraving, cut or plate.

PLATE See *Photoengraving.*

POINT-OF-PURCHASE ADVERTISING *(POP)* Displays prepared for retailers by manufacturers to be used in stores where merchandise is sold. Often designed for customer self-service display units.

POSITION 1. Advertiser's place in a publication or on the page. 2. A company's standing in the market.

POSTER Product sign for display outdoors or in a store window. Must be easily and quickly read at a distance.

PREFERRED POSITION Advertising space usually contracted for an extended period and at an increased cost. Sometimes granted to larger schedules as an inducement. Sometimes available on a rotation basis among advertisers. Top of page, next to reading matter, back page (of a newspaper), inside cover (of a magazine), or a special interest page, such as fashion are examples. See *Position.*

PRESS KIT Organized folder which usually contains press release(s), photographs, fact sheet(s) for distribution to the press for publicity purposes.

PRESS RELEASE In *publicity,* typewritten story ready for an editor, complete in details, facts, and in a format which makes acceptance by the editor easy to get into print.

PRIMARY MARKET LEVEL The basic group in the production cycle and marketing process, manufacturers of fabrics and producers of raw materials.

PRIME TIME In *television,* the hours when maximum audience is viewing, usually 7 to 11 P.M. The Midwest prime time is considered 6 to 10 P.M. See *Drive Time.*

PRIVATE BRAND Trademark or label of a retailer on products exclusive in his store(s). Used extensively by chains and by larger stores. See *House Brand.*

PROCESS PLATES See *Four-Color Process.*

PROCESS PRINTING Letterpress color printing which uses process plates. See *Four-Color Process.*

PRODUCT ADVERTISING Designed to sell products with immediate results. Includes identification and description of merchandise and price, as opposed to institutional advertising.

PRODUCTION (In *advertising*) The mechanical processes in preparation of an advertisement: layout, paste-up, typography, plates.

PROFILE Detailed study of an audience. Usually concerns size, sex, education, income, reading and viewing habits, lifestyle.

PROMOTION *(Sales Promotion)* 1. Any nonpersonal activity used to influence the sale or acceptance of merchandise, services, or ideas. 2. More generally, the total of all selling activities, personal selling, advertising, display, publicity, special events.

PROMOTION MIX Assortment of activities designed to effect sales. The development of details and where emphasis is planned. Integrated activities.

PROOF Copy of an advertisement *before* it is printed. Many proofs are made so that every person and department involved in the advertisement has the opportunity to check for accuracy before the ad is actually run. Corrections are made before the ad appears in print in a publication.

PSYCHOGRAPHICS Analysis and evaluation of consumers' motivations, attitudes, needs, lifestyles, and characteristics for the purpose of marketing planning and strategy.

PUBLIC RELATIONS Any and every contact of an organization with anyone at any time. Also a department responsible for such effort. Policies and direction are top level responsibilities, to survey public opinion and design programs to improve relations with a public.

PUBLICITY Unsponsored by source, non-paid messages, verbal or written in public information media about a company, its policies, personnel, activities or services.

PUBLICITY DIRECTOR The person in charge of the publicity segment of a company's program for promotion.

PULSE Recall media service which is used to measure audience reading or viewing recall of data or impressions which occur during a survey period.

R.A.B. *(Radio Advertising Bureau)* Promotion organization for the radio industry.

RATE CARD List of information issued by a medium. Contains advertising costs, issue dates, closing dates (when all material must be in), cancellation dates and circulation information. Issued by both print and electronic media.

RATING Comparative measurement of the popularity of a radio or television station. Determined by the percentage of total audience tuned in to that station at a specific time period.

RATING POINT One percent of the homes in a measured area whose sets are tuned to a station. Used for comparing of spot stations. See *Gross Rating Points.*

REACH Total actual coverage of a medium.

READERSHIP The number of people who read a publication, not necessarily the count of subscribers: the entire potential audience.

RECALL Measurement of impression of an advertisement or series of advertisements which the reader, listener, or viewer can remember.

REGISTERED *(Trademark)* The act of recording a trademark with the office of the Commissioner of Patents, to prevent imitation.

REMOTE DISPLAY Any nonpersonal showing, away from the point-of-sale, such as in an airport, hotel lobby, train terminal.

REPRINT Reproduction(s) of an advertisement.

RESEARCH DIRECTOR Person in charge of continued studies for marketing, development of products, or in advertising, studies of media and of advertising results.

RESOURCE Term used by retailers for companies from which merchandise is obtained, such as distributors, manufacturers, or wholesalers.

RETAIL ADVERTISING Advertising placed by a retailer for goods, services or ideas, addressed to ultimate consumers.

RETAIL RATE See *Local Rate.*

R.O.P. *(Run of Paper)* Advertising which can appear in any place, on any page of a newspaper as determined by the paper's managing editor.

R.O.S. *(Run of Schedule)* Commercial announcements which can be broadcast at the station's discretion at any time within the period purchased and specified by the sponsor.

ROUGH In the production of layouts, the first crude sketch to show the basic idea or arrangement of an advertisement.

SALES PROMOTION See *Promotion.*

SALES PROMOTION DIRECTOR The person in charge of all sales promotion activities. Responsible for staff and action to produce results.

SALES PROMOTION PLAN Allocations and timing of all the elements of sales promotion, including all the activities, combined to the point of personal selling for complete integration of efforts.

SAMPLE 1. Distribution of a miniature or full size trial package of a product to introduce it. 2. A study of the characteristics of a representative part, or segment, of an audience to establish a program for promotion. Fixed mathematical numbers can be used. When the study keeps duplicating in findings, sample can be established.

SCHEDULE Advertiser's plan for placement and timing of messages in a given period: week, month or season.

SCREEN A fine cross-ruled sheet used in photomechanical platemaking process to produce tone in advertisement, such as shades of gray. The size and number of dots on a screen deliver different gradations of shading. More dots or fewer to the square inch give different values of gray shadings. See *Halftone.*

SCRIPT Copywriter's written form for a broadcast commercial. Contains not only words, but also technical instructions for video or musical parts.

SELF-MAILER Any direct-mail advertising piece on which the address is printed or written directly on the mailer. No envelope is needed.

SHOW *(Fashion Show)* Formal display of merchandise with a theme, program, music, commentator, script . . . on living and moving models.

SHOWING (of Fashions) Informal display on living and moving models. No particular theme, script, commentator or program; no planned continuity. Usually held in showrooms of manufacturers or in a store's fashion department to show merchandise in use.

SIGNATURE 1. Name of an advertiser. 2. A sound effect or musical bar(s) heard often enough to identify the sponsor.

SIMMONS *(W.R. Simmons and Associates Research Company)* Serves advertisers with reports of media audience exposure and product usage information.

SIMPLIFIED SELLING Presentation of merchandise without the presence of sales people. The use of display, counters, bins, or table to show merchandise in assortment for customer to come into direct contact with the items.

SOUND EFFECTS *(SFX)* Sounds other than words or music in a broadcast, such as a train whistle, creaking or closing door, patter of rain.

SPECIAL EVENTS Specific devices, features, services, sales inducements, exhibits, demonstrations, attractions which influence the sale of merchandise or ideas. Often held for storewide attention.

SPECIALTY ADVERTISING Useful articles, such as ball-point pens or key rings, to which an advertiser adds his name for free distribution. Usually inexpensive items given to potential customers to establish goodwill.

SPLIT RUN Some publications permit alternate advertisements from a single sponsor to be run in each of two halves of the total circulation. Used at times for two different approaches for the same item; other times for two different items. Advertisers use split runs to compare effectiveness of different advertisements. Many magazines and newspapers are known to offer such a plan. Available in many national magazines by areas, or "magazones." Either the product or the copy may be changed according to the plan and mechanical requirements of the magazine.

SPONSOR The organization that orders space or time and pays the bill.

SPOT In *radio* and *television,* the purchase of time from a single station rather than from a network. Used as a term for local exposure, or to denote a short (ten-second) commercial.

SPOT COLOR Usually a limited area of color without any screening; used for emphasis in print advertising, to attract attention.

SPREAD Double-page advertisement on two facing pages. When this occurs in the center pages of a publication, the print may extend into the "gutter." This is called a *center spread.* This involves a higher cost for both plates and space. See *Gutter.*

STANDARD (Newspaper Size) Full size newspapers as opposed to tabloid, e.g. *Chicago Tribune, The New York Times, Los Angeles Times, Wall Street Journal.*

STANDARD RATE AND DATA SERVICE *(SRDS)* 1. A publication which lists rates and discounts of all major media. Kept up-to-date with monthly issues. 2. The publisher of market studies on media and market areas.

STARCH Method of checking advertising recognition and recall as developed and sold as reports by Daniel Starch and staff.

STEREOTYPE A duplicate plate for printing made by pouring molten metal into a matrix.

STORE BRAND See *House Brand.*

STORYBOARD Series of drawings along with audio script to present sequence of scenes for a commercial on television. Instructions are scene-by-scene.

SUBHEAD Small type headline that follows larger type *headline.* Usually contains further information to reader.

TABLOID Newspaper about half the size of a standard-size paper, e.g., New York *Daily News, Women's Wear Daily, (WWD).*

TAG Local retailer's message added to a manufacturer's commercial. Usually ten seconds. See *I.D.*

TARGET AUDIENCE Special group within an audience to which advertising is specifically aimed. Example would be an advertisement in a college publication, addressed to skiers among the student readers.

TARGET MARKET The defined segment of a whole market to which an advertiser directs merchandising, merchandise, and promotion. Can be identified by demographics.

TEAR SHEET Copy of an advertisement *after* publication, torn from the actual publication. Positive proof of publication.

T.G.I. *(Target Group Index)* Print and broadcast exposure measure and product usage data reported by Axiom Research Bureau.

THEME Main sales idea of an advertisement or of a campaign.

TRADE ADVERTISING Advertising directed to wholesale or to retail merchants, or to selling agents, as opposed to consumer audiences.

TRADEMARK See *Registered.* Applies to a whole business organization, not just to a product.

TRADING AREA The geographical region surrounding and including a metropolitan center in which the total population is considered to be prospective customers. This area is naturally considerably larger than the central city zone.

TRANSIT ADVERTISING Advertising on transit vehicles such as buses, subways, taxis. Often also considered advertising in transit stations, depots and terminals.

T.V.B. *(Television Bureau of Advertising)* Promotion organization of the television industry. Offers many services and information to advertisers.

TYPEFACE The design and style of letters in type of a "family" such as Bodoni, Caslon. Usually named for the original designer.

TYPO The trade term for an error in type.

UHF *(Ultra High Frequency)* Higher frequency television stations all of which have shorter ranges than VHF stations. Channels 14 to 83.

VENDOR The seller of merchandise.

VHF *(Very High Frequency)* The most common television station. Channels 2 to 13.

VIDEO The visual element in television.

VIDEOTAPE In *television,* the method of recording on magnetic tape. Both sound and visual elements can be recorded and played back as often as desired, once recorded.

VISUALIZATION The process of interpreting an idea in visual form. The purpose is to transmit the idea. It can be product alone; product in a setting; product in use.

VO *(Voice-over)* Television copy read by an announcer who does not appear on the screen.

WASH ILLUSTRATION Brushwork which produces a softer picture, made with diluted India Ink or water color with a brush. Offers varying gray tones. Halftones must be used to reproduce.

WHITE SPACE Areas in an advertisement where no printing or illustration appear. Uninked areas.

WINDOW DISPLAY At retail stores, areas facing the outside of stores used for selling by showing merchandise or ideas to attract pedestrian traffic. Generally glass enclosed. (Glass enclosed displays inside store are not called "window display." They are interior display.) Often called the "face" of the store. Prestige windows are institutional; selling windows are used for immediate sales results.

ZONE PLAN A plan in advertising which concentrates on a geographical area, usually a limited area and local. Often used by retailers to gain customers from suburban and urban areas.

# Index